FOREVER PANS™

Emeril Everyday:

Easy and Delicious Meals in Your Forever Cookware

© 2021 Tristar Products, Inc

Emeril Everyday: Easy and Delicious Meals in Your Forever Cookware
Copyright © 2021 by Tristar Products, Inc.

All rights reserved. No part of this book may be reproduced or transmitted in any form or by any means, electronic or mechanical, including photocopying, recording, or by any information storage and retrieval system, without written permission from the publisher.

Distributed by Tristar Products, Inc.
Fairfield, NJ 07004

ISBN: 978-1-7333029-2-0

Photography by Matt Wagemann

Printed in China

E-FPANS_CB_TP_ENG_V1_210820

FOREVER PANS™

Table of Contents

Appetizers & Snacks

Breakfast

Sandwiches

Fried Chicken Sandwiches with Buttermilk Ranch Dressing	50		Blue Cheese Burgers with Portobella Bacon	58
Grilled Vegetable Sandwiches with Basil Pesto Mayonnaise	52		Gouda Turkey Burgers with Cilantro Mayonnaise	59
Meatloaf Mix Burgers	53		Muffuletta	61
Chipotle Pulled Pork Grilled Cheese	53		Sliced Steak Sandwich with Tomato–Basil Compote	62
Shrimp Po' Boys	55		Sloppy Joes	65
Grilled Lamb Sliders with Goat Cheese & Aioli	56			

Chicken

Nashville Hot Boneless Fried Chicken	68		Chicken Parmesan	77
Chicken Cordon Bleu	71		Pecan-Crusted Chicken Breast	78
Grilled Chicken Marinated with Lemon, Garlic & Oregano	72		Spatchcocked Chicken Brushed with Basil Pesto	81
Pan-Seared Chicken Breast with Sun-Dried Tomato & Lemon Sauce	74		Paprika Chicken	82
Chicken Etouffee with Steamed Rice	75		Chicken Scarpariello	83

Beef, Veal, Pork & Lamb

Seafood

Soups, Stews & One-Pot Meals

Grains & Vegetables

Dessert

About Emeril Lagasse

Emeril Lagasse is an Emmy-winning television personality, the chef and proprietor of 11 restaurants, a cookbook author, and a philanthropist. He is a James Beard Award winner known for his mastery of Creole and Cajun cuisine, which inspired the development of his "New New Orleans" style.

Chef Emeril is most notable for having appeared on a wide variety of cooking TV shows, including the long-running and highly rated Food Network shows *Emeril Live* and *Essence of Emeril*, and most recently, Amazon's original series *Eat the World with Emeril Lagasse*.

Chef Emeril believes that every home kitchen deserves cookware that offer a wide range of custom cooking capabilities. The Forever Pans are designed to be versatile enough to cook almost anything you can imagine and durable enough to be a staple in your kitchen for years to come.

Emeril's Seasonings

You can make these seasonings and store them in small airtight containers. These recipes yield about ½–¾ cup. Making extra seasonings saves time and money, and you will enjoy having some versatile flavors at the ready in your cooking arsenal.

EMERIL'S ORIGINAL ESSENCE

3 tbsp. dried oregano

3 tbsp. dried basil

2 tbsp. dried parsley

1 tbsp. dried rosemary, marjoram, or sage, rubbed between your fingers

1 tsp. crushed red pepper

2 tsp. onion powder

2 tsp. garlic powder

EMERIL'S CREOLE SEASONING

2 ½ tbsp. paprika

2 tbsp. salt

2 tbsp. garlic powder

1 tbsp. black pepper

1 tbsp. onion powder

1 tbsp. cayenne pepper

1 tbsp. dried leaf oregano

1 tbsp. dried thyme

Equivalency Charts

Dry (Weight) Measurements

Misc.※	Teaspoons	Tablespoons	Ounces	Cups	Grams	Pounds
1 dash	$\frac{1}{16}$ tsp.	—	—	—	—	—
1 pinch/ 6 drops	⅛ tsp.	—	—	—	—	—
15 drops	¼ tsp.	—	—	—	—	—
1 splash	½ tsp.	—	—	—	—	—
—	1 tsp.	⅓ tbsp.	⅙ oz	—	—	—
—	3 tsp.	1 tbsp.	½ oz	—	14.3 g	—
—	—	2 tbsp.	1 oz	⅛ cup	28.3 g	—
—	—	4 tbsp.	2 oz	¼ cup	56.7 g	—
—	—	5 ⅓ tbsp.	2.6 oz	⅓ cup	75.6 g	—
—	—	8 tbsp.	4 oz	½ cup	113.4 g	—
—	—	12 tbsp.	6 oz	¾ cup	170.1 g	—
—	—	16 tbsp.	8 oz	1 cup	226.8 g	½ lb
—	—	32 tbsp.	16 oz	2 cups	453.6 g	1 lb
—	—	64 tbsp.	32 oz	4 cups/1 qt.	907.2 g	2 lb

※ Dash, pinch, drop, and splash are subjective measurements that have no formally agreed-upon definition.

Doneness Temperatures

Rare	125° F/52° C
Medium-rare	135° F/57° C
Medium	145° F/63° C
Medium-well	155° F/68° C
Well	165° F/74° C

Liquid (Volume) Measurements

Fluid Ounces	Tablespoons	Cups	Milliliter/ Liters	Pints	Quarts	Gallons
1 fl oz	2 tbsp.	⅛ cup	30 ml	—	—	—
2 fl oz	4 tbsp.	¼ cup	60 ml	—	—	—
4 fl oz	8 tbsp.	½ cup	125 ml	—	—	—
8 fl oz	16 tbsp.	1 cup	250 ml	—	—	—
12 fl oz	—	1 ½ cups	375 ml	—	—	—
16 fl oz	—	2 cups	500 ml	1 pint	—	—
32 fl oz	—	4 cups	1 L	2 pints	1 qt.	—
128 fl oz	—	16 cups	4 L	8 pints	4 qts.	1 gallon

Abbreviations

Term	Dry & Liquid	Abbreviation
cup	usually liquid	—
fluid ounce	only liquid	fl oz.
gallon	dry or liquid	—
inch	-	in.
ounce	dry	oz.
pint	dry or liquid	—
pound	dry	lb
quart	dry or liquid	qt./qts.
teaspoon	dry or liquid	tsp.
tablespoon	dry or liquid	tbsp.

Appetizers & Snacks

✳Pictured here

Mexican Chorizo Deviled Eggs

MAKES 24

INGREDIENTS

12 large eggs

½ lb fresh chorizo

½ cup mayonnaise

1 tsp. Creole mustard

¼ tsp. salt

paprika, to sprinkle on top

chopped chives, for garnish

DIRECTIONS

1. In the Stock Pot, add the eggs and cover them with water. Bring to a boil on the stove top and cook for 6 minutes.

2. Turn off the heat and cover the pan for 15 minutes.

3. Run cold water over the eggs.

4. In the Fry Pan, add the chorizo and cook until browned and crumbly.

5. Drain off any excess rendered fat. Let the chorizo cool and then chop the chorizo.

6. Peel the eggs and cut them in half. Remove the yolk and mix the yolk together with the mayonnaise, mustard, and salt.

7. Use a piping bag to fill the white part of the eggs with the yolk mixture.

8. Sprinkle the eggs with the chorizo, paprika, and chives before serving.

TIP: For the perfect hard-boiled eggs, bring the water and eggs to a boil for 1 minute. Then, shut off the heat, cover the pan, and let sit for 13 minutes before cooling and peeling.

Clam Cakes

MAKES ABOUT 36

INGREDIENTS

2 ¼ cups chopped fresh clams

BATTER

1 ½ cups all-purpose flour

1 ½ tsp. baking powder

½ tsp. salt

½ tsp. Emeril's Original Essence seasoning, plus more for dusting

⅛ tsp. ground cayenne pepper

1 large egg, beaten

½ cup milk

½ cup clam juice

3 tbsp. chopped shallots

1 tbsp. finely chopped green onions

1 tbsp. minced parsley

1 tsp. minced garlic

———————

vegetable oil, for frying

TARTAR SAUCE

1 cup mayonnaise

2 tbsp. chopped green onions or scallions (green part only)

2 tbsp. drained sweet pickle relish

1 tbsp. drained capers (chopped if large)

1 tbsp. minced fresh parsley leaves

2 tsp. Dijon mustard

1 tsp. fresh lemon juice

½ tsp. minced fresh tarragon

¼ tsp. salt

¼ tsp. ground cayenne pepper

———————

chopped parsley leaves, for garnish

lemon wedges, for garnish

DIRECTIONS

1. Drain the clams while making the batter.

2. Into a large bowl, sift the flour, baking powder, salt, Essence seasoning, and cayenne pepper. Add the egg, milk, and clam juice and mix to make a thick batter. Fold in the clams, shallots, green onions, parsley, and garlic.

3. In the High-Sided Fry Pan, add enough oil to reach halfway up the sides of the pan. Heat the oil to 350° F/177° C. When the oil is hot, add batches of the Batter (about 1 tbsp. at a time). Turn the batter once while cooking. Cook until golden brown (3–4 minutes).

4. Remove the clam cakes with a slotted spoon, drain on paper towels, and season lightly with Essence seasoning.

5. In a bowl, combine the Tartar Sauce ingredients.

6. Arrange the clam cakes on a large platter with the Tartar Sauce in a bowl in the center of the platter. Garnish with the parsley and serve with the lemon wedges on the side.

Cauliflower Mac & Cheese Balls

MAKES 24

INGREDIENTS

1 head cauliflower, chopped

1 cup heavy cream

1 ½ cups shredded cheddar

1 tbsp. cornstarch

½ tsp. ground white pepper

1 ½ tsp. salt, divided

4 large eggs

½ cup milk

¼ tsp. ground black pepper

3 cups flour

4 cups breadcrumbs

1 tbsp. Emeril's Original Essence seasoning

vegetable or canola oil, for frying

DIRECTIONS

1. Preheat the oven to 400° F/204° C.

2. In the Stock Pot, add the cauliflower. Cover the pot with its lid. When the oven is preheated, place the pot in the oven and cook the cauliflower for 20 minutes. When the cauliflower is done cooking, transfer to a strainer to drain any excess liquid. Reserve the cauliflower.

3. Clean out the Stock Pot and return to the stove top. In the Stock Pot, bring the cream to a simmer.

4. Toss the cheddar and cornstarch together and add to the simmering cream. Whisk until smooth and creamy.

5. Add the cauliflower to the Stock Pot, season with the white pepper and 1 tsp. salt, and mix.

6. Refrigerate the cauliflower mixture in the Stock Pot until firm (about 4 hours).

7. After 4 hours have passed, use a small ice cream scoop to make the cauliflower balls.

8. In a bowl, combine the eggs, milk, ½ tsp. salt, and ¼ tsp. black pepper and mix.

9. Place the flour in a shallow pan.

10. Place the breadcrumbs in a separate shallow pan and season with 1 tbsp. Essence seasoning.

11. Dredge the cauliflower balls in the flour, then the egg mixture, and finally the breadcrumbs.

12. In the High-Sided Fry Pan, add enough oil to reach halfway up the sides of the pan. Heat the oil to 350° F/177° C. When the oil is hot, fry the cauliflower balls until golden. Transfer to paper towels to drain briefly before serving.

Fried Calamari
with Sweet Chili Sauce

SERVES 4

INGREDIENTS

1 lb calamari,
sliced into ¼-inch rings

2 cups buttermilk

1 tbsp. Louisiana hot sauce

2 cups flour

2 tbsp. Emeril's Original
Essence seasoning

canola oil, for frying

¾ cup sweet chili sauce

DIRECTIONS

1. In a bowl, soak the calamari in the buttermilk and hot sauce. Refrigerate for 4-6 hours.

2. When ready, drain the calamari. In a bowl, combine the flour and Essence seasoning. Toss the calamari in the seasoned flour.

3. In the High-Sided Fry Pan, add enough canola oil to fill the pan halfway. Heat the oil to 375° F/191° C.

4. Use a dry strainer to shake off any excess flour. Fry the calamari in batches until crispy (about 3 minutes). Transfer to paper towels to drain briefly before serving.

5. Serve with the sweet chili sauce.

TIP: To coat in flour in batches, use a strainer to shake off any excess flour.

Fried Artichoke
with Garlic Aioli   SERVES 6

INGREDIENTS

2 large eggs

¼ cup milk

2 cups breadcrumbs

2 tsp. granulated garlic

2 tsp. granulated onion

¼ cup grated Parmigiano-Reggiano cheese

1 tbsp. chopped parsley

1 tsp. salt

½ tsp. ground black pepper
1 cup flour

10–12 canned or frozen whole artichoke hearts (drained if canned)

canola oil, for frying

QUICK GARLIC AIOLI

¾ cup mayonnaise

juice of ⅓ lemon

½ tsp. lemon zest

2 cloves garlic

DIRECTIONS

1. In a bowl, beat the eggs and milk together. Reserve the egg mixture.

2. In a shallow pan, mix the breadcrumbs with granulated garlic, onion, cheese, parsley, salt, and black pepper. Reserve the seasoned breadcrumbs.

3. Place the flour into a separate bowl.

4. Toss the artichoke hearts in the flour and coat well. Remove from the flour and shake off any excess flour.

5. Dip the floured artichokes into the egg mixture and then into the seasoned breadcrumbs.

6. In the High-Sided Fry Pan, add enough canola oil to fill one third of the pan. Heat the oil to 325° F/163° C (be careful not to overheat the oil. When the oil is hot, fry the breaded artichoke lightly. Transfer to paper towels to drain briefly before serving.

7. In a blender, add all the Quick Garlic Aioli ingredients and pulse until the garlic is chopped. Serve the artichokes with the aioli.

Turkey Meatballs

SERVES 6

INGREDIENTS

MEATBALLS

1 lb ground turkey breast

1 bunch scallions, chopped

2 tbsp. Worcestershire sauce

2 large eggs

½ cup breadcrumbs

2 tbsp. heavy cream

1 tsp. minced garlic

1 tsp. salt

½ tsp. ground black pepper

1 tsp. Emeril's Original
Essence seasoning

3 tbsp. chopped cilantro

SAUCE

½ cup sweet chili sauce

2 tbsp. soy sauce

2 tbsp. barbeque sauce

1 tsp. sriracha

DIRECTIONS

1. Preheat the oven to 375° F/191° C.

2. In a bowl, combine the Meatball ingredients and mix well. Roll the mixture into 1 ½-inch balls. Place the Crisper in the High-Sided Fry Pan and place the meatballs in the Crisper.

3. Place the pan in the oven and cook until the meatballs are done (about 20 minutes).

4. In the Sauce Pot, add all the Sauce ingredients and bring to a boil on the stove top.

5. When the Meatballs and Sauce are ready, toss together and serve.

Zucchini Pancakes
with Chive Sour Cream

MAKES 14 PATTIES

INGREDIENTS

2 zucchinis, shredded

½ onion, minced

1 clove garlic, minced

1 tsp. salt

½ tsp. ground white pepper

1 tbsp. chopped parsley

½ cup flour

½ cup shredded Parmigiano-Reggiano cheese

2 large eggs

canola or vegetable oil, for frying

CHIVE SOUR CREAM

½ cup sour cream

2 tbsp. mayonnaise

½ tsp. salt

¼ tsp. ground black pepper

1 clove garlic, minced

2 tbsp. chopped chives

DIRECTIONS

1. In a bowl, combine the shredded zucchini, onion, garlic, salt, white pepper, and parsley. Sprinkle with flour and cheese.

2. In a separate bowl, beat the eggs and mix them into the zucchini. Form the mixture into 2-inch patties.

3. In the High-Sided Fry Pan, add about ¾ inch of oil. Heat the oil over medium heat on the stove top. When the oil is hot, fry the patties on both sides.

4. In a bowl, combine the Chive Sour Cream ingredients.

5. Top the zucchini pancakes with the Chive Sour Cream and serve.

Beer-Battered Shrimp
with Asian Dipping Sauce

SERVES 4-6

INGREDIENTS

BEER BATTER

1 ½ cups flour

½ tsp. ground cumin

1 tsp. onion powder

½ tsp. ground cayenne pepper

1 tbsp. paprika

12 oz beer

1 large egg

1 tbsp. Worcestershire sauce

1 tsp. Louisiana hot sauce

DIPPING SAUCE

2 tbsp. sweet chili sauce

1 tbsp. rice wine

1 tbsp. plum sauce

1 tbsp. soy sauce

1 tsp. sesame oil

_____

canola oil, for frying

1 lb 21–25-size shrimp, peeled & deveined

DIRECTIONS

1. In a bowl, make the Beer Batter: Add the flour, cumin, onion powder, cayenne pepper, and paprika. Then, add the beer, egg, Worcestershire sauce, and hot sauce and whisk until smooth.

2. In a small bowl, mix the Dipping Sauce ingredients. Reserve the Dipping Sauce.

3. In the High-Sided Fry Pan, add enough canola oil to fill one third of the pan. Heat the oil to 350° F/177° C.

4. Dip the shrimp into the Beer Batter. Shake off any excess batter. When the oil is hot, fry the shrimp in batches. Transfer to paper towels or a wire rack to drain briefly before serving.

5. Serve the shrimp with the Dipping Sauce.

TIP: For a different dipping sauce, try Cognac Mayonnaise: Combine 1 tbsp. cognac with ½ cup mayonnaise.

Pulled Pork Mini Tostados
with Chipotle Mayonnaise   MAKES 24

INGREDIENTS

2 cups pulled pork

½ cup barbeque sauce

vegetable or canola oil,
for frying

8 corn tortillas

CHIPOTLE MAYONNAISE

1 cup mayonnaise

4 canned chipotle chiles
in adobo sauce

_____

4 scallions, chopped

DIRECTIONS

1. In the Sauce Pot, add the pulled pork and
barbeque sauce and heat over medium heat
on the stove top until warm.

2. In the High-Sided Fry Pan, add enough oil to fill
one third of the pan. Heat the oil to 350° F/177° C.

3. Use a 2 ½-inch round cookie cutter to cut
three circles in each of the tortillas to make
24 tortilla circles.

4. When the oil is hot, fry the tortilla circles
until slightly golden. Drain the tortilla circles
on paper towels.

5. Puree the mayonnaise and the chipotles in
a food processor.

6. Place the tortillas on a platter and top with about
1 ½ tbsp. pulled pork on each tortilla. Drizzle with
some Chipotle Mayonnaise and garnish with the
chopped scallions before serving.

TIP: Alternatively, you can
use flour tortillas with cheese
to make quesadillas. Cut into
small triangles, drizzle with
chipotle mayonnaise, and
top with scallions.

Crab Cakes with Corn Salad
& Sriracha Mayo

INGREDIENTS

CRAB CAKES

1 lb lump crab meat, drained well & picked over for any shells

1 large egg

¼ cup mayonnaise

¾ cup cracker crumbs

1 tbsp. Dijon mustard

1 red bell pepper, small diced

1 shallot, minced

1 tsp. seafood seasoning

CORN SALAD

2 ears corn, grilled

juice of ½ lime

2 tbsp. chopped cilantro

½ jalapeño, minced

¼ tsp. salt

¼ tsp. ground black pepper

SRIRACHA MAYONNAISE

½ cup mayonnaise

2 tbsp. sriracha

---

vegetable oil, for frying

flour, for dredging

DIRECTIONS

1. In a bowl, combine the Crab Cakes ingredients and mix gently. Form the mixture into 2-inch patties.

2. Remove the corn from the cob. In a bowl, toss the corn and the rest of the Corn Salad ingredients together. Reserve the Corn Salad.

3. In a separate bowl, combine the Sriracha Mayonnaise ingredients. Reserve the Sriracha Mayonnaise.

4. In the High-Sided Fry Pan, add about 1 inch of vegetable oil. Heat the oil over medium-high heat on the stove top.

5. Dredge the Crab Cakes in flour to coat lightly. When the oil is hot, carefully brown each Crab Cake on both sides. Transfer to paper towels to drain briefly before serving.

6. Place some Sriracha Mayonnaise on each Crab Cake and top with the Corn Salad before serving.

Vietnamese-Style Chicken Wings

SERVES 2

INGREDIENTS

1 lb chicken wings, raw, not frozen, cut into segments & wing tips discarded

canola oil, for frying

SAUCE

⅓ cup fish sauce

½ cup sweet chili sauce

4 scallions, chopped

¼ cup chopped cilantro

1 clove garlic, minced

juice of 2 limes

DIRECTIONS

1. In the High-Sided Fry Pan, add enough canola oil to fill one third of the pan. Heat the oil over high heat on the stove top. When the oil is hot, fry the wings in two batches until golden and well-cooked.

2. In a bowl, combine the Sauce ingredients. Toss the fried wings in the Sauce.

3. When all the wings are fried and tossed in the Sauce, serve.

TIP: For boneless wings, cut a chicken breast into chunks, season with salt and black pepper, dip into flour, fry, and coat with the sauce.

Hot Sausage & Pepper Quesadillas

SERVES 2-4

INGREDIENTS

2 ½ tbsp. olive oil, divided

4 hot sausages (about ¾ lb)

1 red bell pepper, sliced

1 small onion, sliced

1 ½ cups shredded Jack cheese

4 8-inch flour tortillas

¼ cup chopped cilantro

¼ cup plus 1 tbsp. olive oil

DIRECTIONS

1. In the Fry Pan, add 1 tbsp. olive oil. Heat the oil over medium-high heat on the stove top. When the oil is hot, sauté the sausages with the pan covered with its lid until done. Slice and reserve the sausage.

2. Add the pepper and onion and cook until tender.

3. In the High-Sided Fry Pan, add 1 ½ tbsp. olive oil. Heat the oil over medium heat on the stove top. When the oil is hot, place 1 tortilla in the pan, top with ¾ cup cheese; half of the sausage, pepper, onion, and cilantro; and another tortilla. Cook until golden on both on sides and the cheese is melted.

4. Repeat the cooking process to make a second quesadilla.

TIP: Remove the sausage from the casings and cook the meat with the peppers, onions, and add tomato sauce for a different kind of quesadilla.

Breakfast

✳Pictured here

Sweet Potato Hash & Eggs

SERVES 2

INGREDIENTS

2 small sweet potatoes

3 tbsp. grapeseed oil

1 cup small-diced small onion

1 cup diced red pepper

½ tsp. granulated garlic

½ tsp. paprika

1 tsp. salt

½ tsp. ground black pepper

¼ cup chopped cilantro

4 large eggs

red pepper flakes, for garnish

DIRECTIONS

1. Microwave the sweet potatoes for 4 minutes to soften slightly. When the sweet potatoes cool, peel and dice.

2. In the Fry Pan, heat the grapeseed oil over medium heat on the stove top. When the oil is hot, brown the potatoes.

3. Add the onion and pepper and cook until tender.

4. Add the garlic, paprika, salt, black pepper, and cilantro and stir. Top with the eggs, cover the pan with its lid, and cook the eggs.

5. When the eggs are done, top with the red pepper flakes.

TIP: Mix with diced white potatoes instead of all sweet potatoes and top with salsa to spice it up.

Smoked Salmon Benedict
with a Béarnaise Sauce   SERVES 2

INGREDIENTS

6 sprigs tarragon, divided

¼ cup white wine

2 tbsp. cider vinegar

½ shallot, chopped

1 bay leaf

8 peppercorns

2 egg yolks

6 oz unsalted butter, melted & cooled to room temperature

1 tbsp. lemon juice

1 pinch salt

1 pinch ground black pepper

———————

1 tbsp. red wine vinegar

4 large eggs

2 English muffins

6 oz smoked salmon

DIRECTIONS

1. Lightly chop 4 tarragon sprigs. In the Sauce Pot, add the chopped tarragon, wine, vinegar, shallot, bay leaf, and peppercorns. Bring to a boil on the stove top and reduce until about 2 tbsp. of liquid is left. Strain and let cool to room temperature.

2. In a bowl, whisk the egg yolks and the reduced tarragon mixture for about 1 minute.

3. Remove and reserve in a stainless steel bowl large enough to fit the rest of the Béarnaise Sauce ingredients and fit in the Sauce Pot (to make a double boiler).

4. Clean out the Sauce Pot. In the Sauce Pot, add 2 cups water over low heat on the stove top and bring to a simmer. Place the bowl with the egg yolk mixture on top and very slowly drizzle the melted butter into the dish while continually whisking until emulsified.

5. Chop the rest of the tarragon. Remove the stainless steel bowl and add the lemon juice, tarragon, salt, and black pepper. Reserve in a warm area while poaching the eggs.

6. Add more water to the Sauce Pot to fill halfway. Bring to a boil on the stove top and then lower to a simmer.

7. Add the wine vinegar and poach the eggs, undisturbed, until the whites are cooked and the yolk is soft (about 4 minutes).

8. Place the English muffins in the Crisper and toast the muffins in the oven's broiler.

9. Divide half of the smoked salmon, 2 poached eggs, and half of the Béarnaise Sauce equally between each English muffin and serve.

Linguiça Frittata

SERVES 4

INGREDIENTS

2 tbsp. olive oil

10 oz diced potatoes

1 onion, sliced

1 red pepper, sliced

½ lb linguiça, sliced

8 large eggs

½ cup heavy cream

1 tsp. salt

½ tsp. ground black pepper

1 tsp. paprika

½ lb provolone, diced

DIRECTIONS

1. Preheat the oven to 350° F/177° C.

2. In the Fry Pan, heat the olive oil over medium-high heat on the stove top. When the oil is hot, add the potatoes and brown lightly.

3. Add the onion, pepper, and linguica and sauté for about 5 minutes.

4. In a bowl, beat the eggs with the heavy cream, salt, black pepper, and paprika. Pour the eggs into the Fry Pan and stir.

5. Add the provolone. Transfer the Fry Pan to the oven and bake until fully cooked (10–15 minutes).

6. Transfer to a platter or cutting board and before serving.

TIP: Linguiça is a Portuguese smoked, cured sausage that goes great with eggs over easy too.

Eggs in a Basket
with Crumbled Chorizo

SERVES 2

INGREDIENTS

4 oz fresh chorizo

¼ cup butter, softened

4 slices white bread

4 large eggs

¼ cup chopped chives

salt, to taste

ground black pepper, to taste

DIRECTIONS

1. In the Fry Pan, cook the chorizo over medium heat on the stove top until browned. Reserve the chorizo. Spoon off and discard any excess fat.

2. Butter both sides of the bread. Use a 2-inch cookie cutter or juice glass to cut a hole in the middle of each bread slice.

3. In the High-Sided Fry Pan, add the bread slices. Place an egg in the center of each bread slice and cook over medium heat on the stove top. When the eggs are partially cooked, flip and top with the crumbled chorizo.

4. Top with the chopped chives and season with the salt and black pepper before serving.

Emeril's Essence
O'Brien Potatoes

SERVES 4

INGREDIENTS

4 potatoes, diced

3 tbsp. olive oil

1 onion, diced small

½ red pepper, diced small

½ green pepper, diced small

2 tsp. Emeril's Original Essence seasoning

DIRECTIONS

1. In the Sauce Pot, add the potatoes and enough water to cover the potatoes. Simmer on the stove top for about 10 minutes.

2. Drain the potatoes well and let cool.

3. In the High-Sided Fry Pan, heat the olive oil over medium-high heat on the stove top. When the oil is hot, brown the potatoes with the onion and peppers.

4. Add the Essence seasoning and stir.

5. Serving suggestion: Serve with eggs and bacon.

Sweet Potato Pancakes
with an Apple Compote

SERVES 4-6

INGREDIENTS

PRALINE SYRUP

1 cup syrup

⅓ cup chopped pecans

PANCAKE BATTER

½ cup sweet potato puree

1 ½ cups buttermilk

1 tsp. cinnamon

¼ tsp. nutmeg

1 egg

1 ⅓ cups flour

2 tsp. baking powder

2 tbsp. sugar

¼ tsp. salt

—————————

2 tbsp. butter

APPLE COMPOTE

1 tbsp. butter

1 apple, cored & sliced

1 tbsp. sugar

1 tbsp. lemon juice

DIRECTIONS

1. In the Sauce Pot, add the Praline Syrup ingredients and heat gently over low heat on the stove top for 10 minutes.

2. In a bowl, mix together the sweet potato, egg, and buttermilk.

3. Add the rest of the Pancake Batter ingredients and mix gently until just combined.

4. In the Fry Pan, melt 2 tbsp. butter over medium heat on the stove top. Make three pancakes at a time. Repeat until all the Pancake Batter is used up.

5. When the pancakes are done cooking, melt the butter in the Fry Pan. Add the rest of the Apple Compote ingredients and toss until cooked (about 4 minutes).

6. Serve the pancakes with the Apple Compote and Praline Syrup.

Chaurico, Sweet Mini Pepper & Gouda Omelet

SERVES 1-2

INGREDIENTS

1 tbsp. olive oil

¼ cup chaurico sausage (Portuguese chorizo)

4 sweet mini peppers, seeded & top removed

1 clove garlic, sliced

3 large eggs

1 tbsp. chopped cilantro

3 tbsp. heavy cream

salt, to taste

ground black pepper, to taste

3 slices Gouda, diced

DIRECTIONS

1. In the Fry Pan, heat the olive oil over medium-high heat on the stove top. When the oil is hot, sauté the chaurico and mini peppers.

2. Add the garlic and cook until slightly golden.

3. In a bowl, combine the eggs, cilantro, cream, salt, and black pepper.

4. Lower the heat slightly and push the peppers and chaurico to one side. Pour the eggs into the center of the pan, stir once, spoon the peppers and chaurico on top of the eggs, and angle the pan so that the eggs coat the entire bottom.

5. Top with the Gouda and carefully fold the omelet over to cover the chaurico, peppers, and cheese. Cook until the egg is cooked.

6. Slide the omelet onto a plate to serve.

TIP: You can use linguiça or chorizo if you can't find chaurico. Add chopped herbs to the eggs for additional flavor.

Stuffed French Toast
with Raspberry Jam & Mascarpone SERVES 4

INGREDIENTS

FRENCH TOAST BATTER

4 large eggs

¼ cup heavy cream

½ tsp. cinnamon

1 tsp. vanilla extract

¼ cup flour

---

8 slices bread

¾ cup mascarpone

¾ cup raspberry jam

powdered sugar

DIRECTIONS

1. In a bowl, beat together the French Toast Batter ingredients. Reserve the batter.

2. In the High-Sided Fry Pan, add enough oil to fill the pan one quarter full. Heat the oil over medium-high heat on the stove top.

3. Spread the mascarpone on 4 bread slices and raspberry jam on the other 4 slices. Sandwich the raspberry and mascarpone slices together to make four sandwiches. Cut the sandwiches in halves or quarters.

4. Dip the sandwiches into the French Toast Batter. Working in batches, add the sandwiches to the pan and cook both sides until golden.

5. Serve the stuffed French toast with the powdered sugar.

TIP: You can change jams to any flavor you like, and you can use cream cheese instead of mascarpone.

Spaghetti Omelet

SERVES 4-6

INGREDIENTS

½ lb spaghetti

6 large eggs

¼ cup heavy cream

¾ cup grated Parmigiano-Reggiano cheese

1 tsp. salt

½ tsp. ground black pepper

3 tbsp. olive oil, divided

1 zucchini, diced

1 clove garlic, minced

DIRECTIONS

1. In the Stock Pot, cook the spaghetti until al dente. Drain and set aside to cool.

2. In a large bowl, mix the eggs, cream, cheese, salt, and black pepper.

3. In the Fry Pan, heat 1 tbsp. olive oil over medium-high heat on the stove top. When the oil is hot, sauté the zucchini with the garlic. Set aside to cool.

4. In a bowl, mix together the spaghetti, egg mixture, and the cooled zucchini.

5. Preheat the oven 375° F/191° C.

6. Clean the Fry Pan. In the Fry Pan, heat 2 tbsp. olive oil over medium heat on the stove top. When the oil is hot, add the spaghetti mixture and sauté for 5 minutes. Then, flip and sauté for another 4 minutes.

7. Transfer the Fry Pan to the oven and bake for about 8 minutes.

8. Let rest for about 5 minutes before transferring to a platter or cutting board, cutting, and serving.

Skillet Crumb Cake

SERVES 6

INGREDIENTS

1 ½ sticks butter

¾ cup sugar

2 large eggs

2 tsp. vanilla extract

2 cups flour

2 tsp. baking powder

½ tsp. salt

½ cup buttermilk

½ cup sour cream

CRUMB TOPPING

1 stick butter

¾ cup flour

¾ cup brown sugar

1 tsp. cinnamon

DIRECTIONS

1. Preheat the oven to 350° F/177° C.

2. Use a mixer to cream the butter and sugar until light and fluffy. Add the eggs and vanilla and mix well.

3. In a bowl, mix together the flour, baking powder, and salt.

4. In a separate bowl, combine the buttermilk and sour cream.

5. Alternate adding the flour mixture and buttermilk–sour cream mixture to the butter mixture until just mixed.

6. Pour the batter into the Fry Pan.

7. In a mixing bowl, combine the Crumb Topping ingredients until a crumb-like texture is reached. Sprinkle the Crumb Topping over the batter.

8. Transfer the Fry Pan to the oven and bake until a toothpick inserted into the center of the cake comes out clean (35–40 minutes).

TIP: For leftovers, heat the crumb cake in the fry pan with butter to make toasty.

Sandwiches

❋Pictured here

Fried Chicken Sandwiches
with Buttermilk Ranch Dressing

MAKES 6
SANDWICHES

INGREDIENTS

RANCH DRESSING

½ cup buttermilk

½ cup mayonnaise

1 tsp. dill, chopped

1 tbsp. parsley, chopped

2 tsp. chopped chives

½ tsp. onion powder

½ tsp. garlic powder

¼ tsp. sea salt

¼ tsp. ground black pepper

½ tsp. dry mustard

_____

1 large egg

½ cup buttermilk

4 tsp. Emeril's Original
Essence seasoning, divided

2 cups flour

6 boneless & skinless
chicken thighs

BURGER TOPPINGS

6 brioche rolls

6 leaves lettuce

6 slices tomato

DIRECTIONS

1. In a bowl, combine the Ranch Dressing ingredients. Reserve in the refrigerator until ready to use.

2. In a separate bowl, combine the egg, buttermilk, and 2 tsp. Essence seasoning.

3. In a third bowl, combine the flour and 2 tsp. Essence seasoning.

4. Dip the chicken into the flour, then into the egg–buttermilk mixture, and into the flour again.

5. On the stove top, fill the High-Sided Fry Pan one third full with oil. Heat the oil to 325° F/163° C. When the oil is hot, fry the chicken on both sides. Cook until an instant-read thermometer inserted into the thickest part of the chicken reads 165° F/74° C.

6. Assemble the sandwiches with the lettuce, tomato, fried chicken, and Ranch Dressing.

TIP: Instead of frying the chicken, you can season with Emeril's Original Essence seasoning and grill the chicken with the Grill Plate and High-Sided Fry Pan over high heat.

Grilled Vegetable Sandwiches
with Basil Pesto Mayonnaise   MAKES 2 SANDWICHES

INGREDIENTS

MARINADE

¼ cup olive oil

2 tbsp. balsamic vinegar

1 shallot, minced

1 tsp. sea salt

½ tsp. ground black pepper

_____

2 ¼ inch-thick slices red onion

2 portobella mushrooms

4 ½ inch-thick zucchini slices

2 ciabatta rolls

2 tbsp. basil pesto

¼ cup mayonnaise

1 roasted red pepper, cut in half

4 slices fresh mozzarella

DIRECTIONS

1. In a bowl, combine the Marinade ingredients. In a shallow pan, add the onion, portobella, and zucchini. Pour the marinade over the vegetables. Cover with plastic wrap and marinate for 1 hour on the counter.

2. Place the Grill Plate in the High-Sided Fry Pan. Heat the Grill Plate over medium heat on the stove top. When the Grill Plate is hot, grill the vegetables in stages until tender. Reserve the vegetables.

3. Brush the excess marinade on the rolls and grill the rolls.

4. In a bowl, combine the pesto and mayonnaise.

5. Assemble the sandwiches: Place 1 tbsp. pesto mayonnaise on the bottom half of each roll and layer half of the vegetables over the pesto mayonnaise. Top with the red pepper and mozzarella. Broil until the cheese is slightly melted. Top with another 1 tbsp. pesto mayonnaise and then the top half of each roll before serving.

TIP: Use panini bread and make a vegetable panini using the Grill Plate in the High-Sided Fry Pan over medium heat.

Meatloaf Mix Burgers

MAKES 6 BURGERS

INGREDIENTS

BURGERS

1 ½ lb meatloaf mix ground meat (pork, veal, and beef)

1 yellow pepper, diced

1 small onion, diced small

3 tbsp. barbeque sauce

2 tbsp. Worcestershire sauce

1 tsp. salt

½ tsp. ground black pepper

_____

¼ cup olive oil

2 cloves garlic, smashed

6 slices Swiss cheese

6 ciabatta rolls

ketchup, for serving

DIRECTIONS

1. In a bowl, combine the meatloaf mix, yellow pepper, onion, barbeque sauce, Worcestershire sauce, salt, and black pepper. Form the mixture into six patties.

2. In a bowl, combine the olive oil and garlic. Reserve the olive oil–garlic mixture.

3. Place the Grill Plate in the Fry Pan. Heat the Grill Plate over medium heat on the stove top. When the Grill Plate is hot, add the patties and grill until fully cooked. Then, top with the Swiss cheese and cook until the cheese is melted. Remove and reserve the patties.

4. Brush the rolls with the olive oil–garlic mixture and grill the rolls.

5. Assemble the burgers and top with ketchup.

Chipotle Pulled Pork Grilled Cheese

MAKES 2 SANDWICHES

INGREDIENTS

¾ cup pulled pork

3 tbsp. chipotle barbeque sauce

¼ cup butter, softened

4 slices bread

8 slices Pepper Jack

¼ red onion, sliced thinly

DIRECTIONS

1. In the Sauce Pot, place the pork and barbeque sauce and reheat over medium heat on the stove top.

2. Butter one side of each bread slice. Place two bread slices in the High-Sided Fry Pan on the stove top. Top each bread slice in the pan with half of the cheese, half of the meat, and half of the onion. Top with the other two bread slices. Brown the sandwiches lightly on both sides over medium heat until the cheese is melted.

Shrimp Po' Boys MAKES 6 SANDWICHES

INGREDIENTS

1 lb 21–25-size shrimp

4 tsp. Emeril's Original Essence seasoning, divided

1 cup flour

½ cup finely ground cornmeal

½ cup buttermilk

1 tbsp. hot sauce

RED REMOULADE SAUCE

⅓ cup mayonnaise

2 tbsp. ketchup

2 tbsp. finely chopped celery

1 tbsp. finely chopped yellow onions

1 tbsp. finely chopped green onions (green parts only)

1 tbsp. Creole mustard (or other hot, whole-grain mustard)

1 ½ tsp. red wine vinegar

1 ½ tsp. rice wine vinegar

1 ½ tsp. paprika

1 ½ tsp. minced fresh parsley

1 tsp. prepared horseradish

1 tsp. hot red pepper sauce

½ tsp. minced garlic

———————

2 cups shredded lettuce

18 tomato slices

18 pickle chips

6 club rolls

DIRECTIONS

1. Season the shrimp with 2 tsp. Essence seasoning.

2. In a bowl, combine the flour and cornmeal with 2 tsp. Essence seasoning. In a separate bowl, combine the buttermilk and hot sauce. Dip the shrimp in the buttermilk–hot sauce mixture and then the flour–cornmeal mixture.

3. On the stove top, fill the High-Sided Fry Pan one third full with oil. Heat the oil to 350° F/177° C. Fry the shrimp in the oil until golden. Reserve the shrimp.

4. In a bowl, combine the Red Remoulade Sauce ingredients and whisk lightly to blend. Store in an airtight container and refrigerate until ready to use.

5. Assemble the sandwiches with ⅓ cup lettuce, 3 tomato slices, 3 pickle chips, and 3 shrimp between each club roll. Top with the Red Remoulade Sauce before serving.

TIP: Replace the shrimp with oysters to make an Oyster Po' Boy.

Grilled Lamb Sliders
with Goat Cheese & Aioli   MAKES 6

INGREDIENTS

1 lb ground lamb

2 sprigs tarragon, chopped

1 shallot, minced

2 tbsp. soy sauce

½ tsp. ground black pepper

AIOLI

1 egg yolk

1 tbsp. Dijon mustard

½ clove garlic

juice of ⅓ lemon

¾ cup olive oil

½ tsp. salt

2 tbsp. parsley

———————

½ cup goat cheese

6 slider rolls

⅓ cup butter, softened

DIRECTIONS

1. In a bowl, combine the lamb, tarragon, shallot, soy sauce, and black pepper. Form the mixture into six patties. Reserve the patties.

2. In a food processor, add the egg yolk, mustard, garlic and lemon juice. Turn the food processor on and slowly drizzle the olive oil into the yolk mixture to emulsify.

3. Add the salt and parsley and pulse until the parsley is chopped.

4. Place the Grill Plate in the High-Sided Fry Pan. Heat the Grill Plate over medium-high heat on the stove top. When the Grill Plate is hot, add the patties and cook until the desired doneness is reached.

5. Top the burgers with the goat cheese and cover the pan with its lid for 1 minute to soften slightly.

6. Brush the rolls with the butter. Place the rolls in the Crisper and toast the rolls in the oven's broiler.

7. To assemble the sliders, Place 1 tbsp. Aioli on the bottom of each roll, top with the patties, and top with the top half of each roll.

Blue Cheese Burgers
with Portobella Bacon   MAKES 6 BURGERS

INGREDIENTS

PORTOBELLA BACON

3 portobella mushrooms,
cut ¼ inch thick

2 tbsp. liquid aminos

1 tsp. liquid smoke

1 tsp. brown sugar

1 tsp. paprika

BURGERS

1 ½ lb ground chuck

1 tsp. salt

½ tsp. ground black pepper

½ cup crumbled blue cheese

_____

1 stick butter, softened

6 brioche rolls

lettuce, for serving

tomato slices, for serving

DIRECTIONS

1. In a bowl, toss the portabella slices, liquid aminos, liquid smoke, brown sugar, and paprika. Marinate for 1 hour in the refrigerator.

2. Preheat the oven to 350° F/177° C.

3. Place the portabella slices on the Crisper. Place the Crisper in the oven and cook until crispy.

4. Combine the ground chuck, salt, and black pepper. Divide the mixture into six patties.

5. Place the Grill Plate in the High-Sided Fry Pan. Heat the Grill Plate over medium heat on the stove top. When the Grill Plate is hot, grill the patties.

6. Top the patties with the blue cheese and cover the pan with its lid for 1 minute to melt the cheese.

7. Butter the rolls. Place the rolls in the Crisper and toast the rolls in the oven's broiler.

8. Place the burgers on the rolls and top with the Portabella Bacon, lettuce, and tomato slices.

Gouda Turkey Burgers
with Cilantro Mayonnaise MAKES 6 BURGERS

INGREDIENTS

BURGER

1 ½ lb ground turkey breast

2 egg whites

2 tbsp. extra virgin olive oil

3 tbsp. chopped cilantro

1 shallot, minced

1 tbsp. soy sauce

½ tsp. ground black pepper

1 cup shredded Gouda

CILANTRO MAYONNAISE

⅛ cup chopped cilantro

1 shallot, minced

½ cup mayonnaise

juice of ½ lime

_____

1 stick butter

4 brioche rolls

6 leaves Bibb lettuce

6 slices tomato

DIRECTIONS

1. In a bowl, combine the Burger ingredients. Form the mixture into six patties.

2. Place the Grill Plate in the High-Sided Fry Pan. Heat the Grill Plate over medium heat on the stove top. When the Grill Plate is hot, grill the patties.

3. In a small bowl, combine the Cilantro Mayonnaise ingredients.

4. Butter the rolls. Place the rolls in the Crisper and toast the rolls in the oven's broiler.

5. When the patties are fully cooked, place on the rolls with the lettuce, tomato slices, and mayonnaise.

TIP: Make a patty melt: Caramelize onions and change the bread to rye. Top the buttered rye bread with cheese, the cooked patty, more cheese, cilantro mayo, and the other piece of buttered rye and grill with the Grill Plate and High-Sided Fry Pan.

Muffuletta

MAKES 4–6

INGREDIENTS

OLIVE SALAD

¼ cup green olives
with pimentos

¼ cup Kalamata olives, pitted

6 artichoke quarters

½ clove garlic

¼ cup extra virgin olive oil

2 tbsp. flat-leaf parsley

_____

1 baguette

4 oz capicola, sliced

4 oz soppressata, sliced

4 oz provolone, sliced

4 oz mortadella, sliced

DIRECTIONS

1. Preheat the oven to 375° F/191° C.

2. In a food processor, pulse the olives, artichokes, garlic, extra virgin olive oil, and parsley until chopped.

3. Slice the baguette, hollow out the bottom half, and fill with the Olive Salad.

4. Layer each meat and cheese on top of the Olive Salad. Top with the top half of the baguette.

5. Cut the sandwich in half and place in the High-Sided Fry Pan. Transfer the pan to the oven and cook for 5–8 minutes to melt the cheese.

TIP: Instead of using the cold cuts, use grilled vegetables to make this recipe vegetarian.

Sliced Steak Sandwich
with Tomato–Basil Compote

SERVES 4-6

INGREDIENTS

2 12-oz New York strip steaks

½ tsp. sea salt

½ tsp. coarsely ground
black pepper

2 tbsp. olive oil

TOMATO–BASIL COMPOTE

2 Roma tomatoes, diced

½ shallot, minced

½ clove garlic, minced

8 basil leaves, chopped

3 tbsp. extra virgin olive oil

1 tsp. red wine vinegar

1 pinch salt

1 pinch freshly ground
black pepper

1 pinch sugar

_____

1 baguette, sliced in half

DIRECTIONS

1. Season the steaks with the salt and black pepper.

2. In the Fry Pan, heat the olive oil over high heat on the stove top. When the oil is hot, add the steaks and sear until the desired doneness is reached. Remove and reserve the steaks.

3. In a bowl, toss the Tomato–Basil Compote ingredients.

4. Place some of the compote on the bottom half of the baguette. Slice the steak and layer it on top of the compote. Top with the rest of the compote and the top half of the baguette. Slice the sandwich before serving.

TIP: You can use chicken instead of steak and add fresh mozzarella.

Sloppy Joes

SERVES 6-8

INGREDIENTS

SLOPPY JOES

2 tsp. olive oil

2 lb ground beef

1 small onion, minced

1 green pepper, diced small

2 tbsp. Worcestershire sauce

2 tbsp. brown sugar

1 tbsp. chili powder

1 tsp. onion powder

1 tsp. garlic powder

2 tbsp. apple cider

1 cup ketchup

2 tbsp. yellow mustard

¾ cup water

_____

6-8 hamburger rolls

DIRECTIONS

1. In the High-Sided Fry Pan, heat the olive oil over high heat on the stove top. When the oil is hot, add the beef and cook for 5 minutes.

2. Add the onion and pepper and cook until tender.

3. Add the rest of the ingredients except the rolls and simmer for about 10 minutes.

4. Evenly divide the Sloppy Joes between the hamburger rolls.

TIP: You can use ground turkey or chicken instead of ground beef or top with macaroni and cheese and place into the oven for a skillet dinner.

Chicken

❋Pictured here

Nashville Hot Boneless Fried Chicken

SERVES 4

INGREDIENTS

8 boneless chicken thighs, with skin

2 cups buttermilk

2 large eggs

2 tbsp. Louisiana hot sauce

canola or vegetable oil, for frying, divided

4 cups flour

2 tbsp. Emeril's Original Essence seasoning

NASHVILLE HOT OIL

1 tsp. granulated garlic

½ tsp. granulated onion

1 tbsp. paprika

1 tsp. cumin

1 tsp. coriander

1 tbsp. ground cayenne pepper

2 tbsp. brown sugar

DIRECTIONS

1. In a bowl, mix the eggs, buttermilk, and hot sauce. Refrigerate the chicken in the bowl overnight.

2. In a shallow pan, combine the flour and Essence seasoning.

3. Fill the High-Sided Fry Pan one third full with the oil and heat the oil to 350° F/177° C over high heat on the stove top.. When the oil is hot, turn the heat down slightly. Dip the chicken into the flour and then fry in the oil, turning if necessary, until an instant-read thermometer inserted into the thickest part of the chicken reads 160° F/71° C. Transfer the fried chicken to the Crisper or to paper towels to drain briefly before serving. Reserve ½ cup of the oil.

4. In a bowl, mix all the Nashville Hot Oil ingredients.

5. In the Sauce Pot, heat the reserved ½ cup oil over high heat for 3 minutes. Then, remove the pot from the heat and then add the Nashville Hot Oil ingredients to the oil.

6. Brush the chicken with the Nashville Hot Oil before serving

TIP: To make bone-in fried chicken with this recipe, you can cut a whole chicken into eight pieces.

Chicken Cordon Bleu

SERVES 4

INGREDIENTS

4 6-oz chicken breasts, pounded to ¼ inch thick

2 oz sliced Swiss cheese

2 oz sliced ham

3 large eggs, beaten

2 tbsp. milk

1 cup flour

2 cup breadcrumbs

1 tbsp. Emeril's Original Essence seasoning

¼ cup grated Parmesan cheese

QUINOA PILAF

1 tbsp. olive oil

1 tbsp. butter

1 shallot, minced

¾ cup quinoa

1 ¾ cups chicken broth

1 sprig thyme

1 bay leaf

½ tsp. salt

¼ tsp. ground white pepper

SAUCE

2 tbsp. butter

2 tbsp. flour

1 cup milk

1 bay leaf

1 tsp. Dijon mustard

¼ cup Parmesan cheese

salt, to taste

ground white pepper, to taste

DIRECTIONS

1. Lay the chicken on a cutting board. Divide the Swiss cheese and ham into four portions and evenly layer them on top of the chicken. Roll the chicken and then cover the chicken in plastic wrap tightly. Refrigerate for 1 hour.

2. To make the Quinoa Pilaf: In the Sauce Pot, heat the olive oil and melt the butter over medium heat on the stove top. When the oil is hot and the butter is melted, sauté the shallot for 2 minutes.

3. Add the quinoa and coat with the oil and shallots. Add the broth, thyme, bay leaf, salt, and white pepper and simmer for 20 minutes.

4. To make the Sauce: In the Fry Pan, melt the butter over medium heat on the stove top. When the butter is melted, add the flour. Cook, stirring for several minutes, to make a blond roux.

5. Slowly add the milk and whisk until creamy. Add the bay leaf and mustard and simmer for about 20 minutes.

6. Add the Parmesan and season with the salt and white pepper. Keep the Sauce warm.

7. In a bowl, beat the eggs and milk.

8. In a shallow pan, add the flour.

9. In a separate shallow pan, mix the breadcrumbs, Essence seasoning, and grated Parmesan.

10. Remove the plastic wrap from the chicken. Dust the chicken with the flour, then dip the chicken into the egg mixture, and finally coat the chicken well with the seasoned breadcrumbs. Repeat until all the chicken is breaded.

11. In the High-Sided Fry Pan, heat 3 inches of canola oil over medium heat on the stove top. When the oil is hot, fry the chicken on all sides until golden and an instant-read thermometer inserted into the thickest part of the chicken reads 160° F/71° C.

12. Drizzle the Sauce over the chicken and serve with the Quinoa Pilaf on the side.

Grilled Chicken Marinated with Lemon, Garlic & Oregano

SERVES 2

INGREDIENTS

2 6-oz chicken breasts

MARINADE

juice of 1 lemon

1 clove garlic, minced

3 sprigs fresh oregano, chopped

½ tsp. salt

¼ tsp. ground black pepper

3 tbsp. extra virgin olive oil

SALAD

4 cups salad greens

¼ cup shredded carrots

2 radishes, sliced

10 cherry tomatoes, halved

4 thin slices red onion

¼ cup cucumber slices

½ cup feta cheese

DRESSING

⅓ cup extra virgin olive oil

3 tbsp. balsamic vinegar

¼ tsp. salt

¼ tsp. freshly ground
black pepper

DIRECTIONS

1. In a shallow glass or ceramic pan, combine the Marinade ingredients. Coat the chicken in the Marinade and refrigerate for at least 4 hours.

2. Place the Grill Plate in the High-Sided Fry Pan. Heat the Grill Plate over high heat on the stove top. When the Grill Plate is hot, grill the chicken on both sides until an instant-read thermometer inserted into the thickest part of the chicken reads 160° F/71° C.

3. In a bowl, mix the Salad ingredients.

4. In a small bowl, whisk together the Dressing ingredients.

5. Toss the Salad with the Dressing. Slice the chicken and serve together.

TIP: The chicken can marinate for a couple of days and still grill very well and taste delicious.

Pan-Seared Chicken Breast
with Sun-Dried Tomato & Lemon Sauce   SERVES 2

INGREDIENTS

RICE PILAF

1 tbsp. olive oil

1 tbsp. butter

½ small onion, diced

1 cup rice

1 bay leaf

1 sprig thyme

1 ¾ cups chicken stock

1 pinch salt

1 pinch ground black pepper

―――――――――――

2 8-oz chicken breasts,
sliced into cutlets

1 tsp. salt

½ tsp. ground black pepper

2 tbsp. olive oil

2 cloves garlic, sliced thinly

¼ cup white wine

6 sun-dried tomatoes, cut in half

1 cup chicken stock

2 tbsp. butter

10 basil leaves, chopped

juice of 1 lemon wedge

DIRECTIONS

1. In the Sauce Pot, heat 1 tbsp. olive oil and melt 1 tbsp. butter over medium heat on the stove top. When the oil is hot and the butter is melted, add the onion and sauté for 2 minutes. Add the rice and coat.

2. Add the rest of the Rice Pilaf ingredients. Bring to a boil and cover the pot with its lid.

3. Reduce to a simmer and cook until all the liquid is absorbed (18–20 minutes).

4. Season the chicken with the salt and black pepper. In the High-Sided Fry Pan, heat the olive oil over high heat on the stove top. When the oil is hot, sear the chicken until golden on both sides. Remove and reserve the chicken.

5. Add the garlic to the High-Sided Fry Pan and sauté until slightly golden.

6. Add the wine and tomatoes and reduce until the wine is almost gone.

7. Add the stock and reduce by half.

8. Add the butter, basil, lemon juice, and chicken. Coat the chicken with the sauce and adjust the seasoning if necessary.

9. Serve the chicken over the Rice Pilaf.

TIP: You can also make this recipe with boneless, skinless chicken thighs.

Chicken Etouffee with Steamed Rice

SERVES 4

INGREDIENTS

ROUX

¾ cup canola or vegetable oil

¾ cup flour

_____

4 6–8-oz boneless &
skinless chicken breasts

2 tbsp. plus 2 tsp. Emeril's Creole
seasoning, or to taste, divided

2 tbsp. canola or vegetable oil

1 onion, sliced

1 green bell pepper, chopped

1 rib celery, chopped

4 garlic cloves, chopped finely

24 oz dark beer

2 cups chicken stock

3 tbsp. Worcestershire sauce

1 tbsp. hot pepper sauce

4 bay leaves

salt, to taste

4 cups steamed white rice

4 green onions, sliced

DIRECTIONS

1. In the Sauce Pot, add ¾ cup oil and the flour. Cook over medium-low heat, stirring constantly, to make the Roux. Keep stirring continually and continue cooking until the Roux is nutty brown. When the Roux has reached the desired color, transfer to a heatproof bowl and set aside to cool. Reserve the Roux.

2. Season the chicken breasts with 1 tbsp. Creole seasoning.

3. In the High-Sided Fry Pan, heat 2 tbsp. oil over high heat on the stove top. When the oil is hot, add the onion, bell pepper, celery, and garlic and sauté until the onions are tender.

4. Add the Roux and stir for 3 minutes.

5. Slowly add the beer and stock while whisking constantly to avoid forming lumps. Bring to a boil.

6. Add the chicken breasts, Worcestershire sauce, hot pepper sauce, bay leaves, salt, and 2 tsp. Creole seasoning. Reduce the heat to medium and simmer for 20–30 minutes.

7. Serve over the rice topped with the green onions.

TIP: You can also make this recipe with boneless, skinless chicken thighs.

Chicken Parmesan

SERVES 4

INGREDIENTS

MARINARA SAUCE

1 tbsp. olive oil

1 medium onion, chopped finely

3 garlic cloves, minced

1 tsp. Italian seasoning

½ tsp. crushed red pepper flakes

56 oz canned crushed tomatoes

1 cup water

1 tsp. salt, plus more to taste

½ tsp. freshly ground black pepper, plus more to taste

chopped fresh parsley leaves, for serving

grated Parmesan, for serving

extra virgin olive oil, for serving

_____

2 cups seasoned breadcrumbs

¼ cup grated Parmigiano-Reggiano cheese, plus more for garnish

2 large eggs

¼ cup milk

4 6-oz chicken breasts, pounded to ¼ inch thick

1 tsp. salt

½ tsp. ground black pepper

canola or vegetable oil, for frying

4 slices fresh mozzarella

DIRECTIONS

1. In the Sauce Pot, heat the olive oil over medium heat on the stove top. When the oil is hot, sauté the onion and garlic for 3–4 minutes.

2. Add the rest of the Marinara Sauce ingredients and simmer for 20 minutes.

3. In a shallow pan, add the breadcrumbs and Parmigiano-Reggiano and stir.

4. In a bowl, combine the eggs and milk.

5. Season the chicken with the salt and black pepper. Dip the chicken into the egg mixture and then the breadcrumbs. Reserve on a plate until all the chicken is breaded.

6. In the High-Sided Fry Pan, heat about 1 inch of oil over medium-high heat on the stove top. When the oil is hot, sauté the chicken on both sides.

7. Preheat the oven to 400° F/204° C.

8. Clean out the High-Sided Fry Pan. Pour some Marinara Sauce in the bottom of the pan. Place the chicken in a spiral pattern on top of the Marinara Sauce. Top with some more Marinara Sauce and then the mozzarella.

9. Transfer the High-Sided Fry Pan to the oven and cook until the cheese is bubbly.

10. Serving suggestion: Garnish with additional Parmigiano-Reggiano and serve with pasta or vegetables.

TIP: Instead of frying the breaded chicken in oil, you can place it in the Crisper and cook it in an oven heated to 375° F/191° C for 15 minutes.

Pecan-Crusted Chicken Breast

SERVES 2

INGREDIENTS

2 large eggs

1 cup buttermilk

2 cups pecans

2 tbsp. Emeril's Original Essence seasoning

¼ cup flour

2 6-oz chicken breasts, pounded

½ tsp. salt

¼ tsp. ground black pepper

canola oil, for frying

SAUCE

1 shallot, minced

2 tbsp. butter

juice & zest of 1 orange

¾ cup chicken stock

2 tbsp. orange marmalade

1 sprig thyme

¼ tsp. salt

¼ tsp. ground black pepper

roasted butternut squash, for serving

DIRECTIONS

1. In a small bowl, combine the eggs and buttermilk.

2. In a food processor, pulse the pecans, Essence seasoning, and flour until blended to a crumb-like consistency.

3. Season the chicken with the salt and black pepper.

4. Dip the chicken into the egg mixture and then the pecan crust.

5. In the High-Sided Fry Pan, heat about 1 inch of canola oil to over medium heat on the stove top. When the oil is hot, fry the chicken on both sides. Reserve the chicken and clean out the pan.

6. In the High-Sided Fry Pan, sauté the shallot in the butter for 1 minute.

7. Add the rest of the Sauce ingredients and reduce until slightly thickened.

8. Pour the Sauce over the chicken and serve with the roasted butternut squash.

TIP: If you want to try a different flavor, you can change the pecans to almonds.

Spatchcocked Chicken
Brushed with Basil Pesto
SERVES 2

INGREDIENTS

1 4-lb chicken

2 tsp. salt, divided

2 tsp. ground black pepper, divided

2 tbsp. olive oil

8 baby potatoes, halved

2 carrots, cut into chunks

8 cloves garlic

6 mini sweet peppers

2 tbsp. extra virgin olive oil

2 tbsp. basil pesto

DIRECTIONS

1. Spatchcock the chicken: Remove any neck parts and gizzards. Rinse the whole chicken inside and out and pat dry with a paper towel. Place the chicken, breast side down, on a cutting board. Use poultry shears or kitchen scissors to cut along the one side of the chicken's backbone from the tail to the neck. Cut the other side of the backbone in the same way and remove the backbone. Press down on breastbone until the breastbone cracks. Use kitchen scissors to remove the wing tips. Season the chicken with 1 tsp. salt and 1 tsp. black pepper.

2. Preheat the oven to 400° F/204° C.

3. In the High-Sided Fry Pan, heat the olive oil over high heat on the stove top. Sear the chicken, skin side down, until browned.

4. In a bowl, toss the potatoes, carrots, garlic, peppers, extra virgin olive oil, 1 tsp. salt, and 1 tsp. black pepper.

5. Flip the chicken and add the potatoes, garlic, peppers, and carrots to the pan.

6. Transfer the pan to the oven and cook the chicken until an instant-read thermometer inserted into the thickest part of the chicken reads 160° F/71° C and the vegetables are tender (20–30 minutes).

7. Brush the chicken with the pesto before serving.

TIP: To cook this dish more quickly, you can remove the bones from the chicken.

Paprika Chicken

SERVES 4

INGREDIENTS

1 3 ½-lb chicken, cut into 8 pieces

3 tbsp. sweet Hungarian paprika, divided

2 tsp. hot Hungarian paprika, divided

1 tbsp. plus ½ tsp. salt, divided

3 tbsp. butter

1 cup finely chopped yellow onion

2 tsp. minced garlic

½ cup peeled, chopped & seeded tomatoes

1–1 ½ cups chicken stock

½ cup sour cream

SPAETZLE

2 large eggs, beaten slightly

1 ½ cups flour, sifted

½ cup milk

1 tsp. salt

¼ tsp. baking powder

_____

2 tbsp. butter

DIRECTIONS

1. Season the chicken with 2 tbsp. sweet paprika, 1 tsp. hot paprika, and 1 tbsp. salt.

2. In the High-Sided Fry Pan, melt the butter over medium-high heat on the stove top. When the butter is melted, brown the chicken.

3. Add the onion, 1 tsp. sweet paprika, 1 tsp. hot paprika, and ½ tsp. salt and cook while stirring for 2 minutes.

4. Add the garlic and cook for 30 seconds.

5. Add the tomatoes and cook for 1 minute.

6. Add enough stock to cover the chicken and bring to a boil.

7. Lower the heat, cover the pan with its lid, and simmer until the chicken is tender and cooked through (about 30 minutes), adding more stock as needed.

8. Uncover the pan and add the sour cream. Cook gently until incorporated and warmed through (about 2 minutes). Season to taste.

9. In a bowl, combine the Spaetzle ingredients to make a batter.

10. Fill the Stock Pot three quarters full with water, add 1 tbsp. salt, and bring to a boil over high heat on the stove top.

11. Place a colander over the pan. Pour about one quarter of the Spaetzle batter into the colander and press the batter through the holes into the hot water.

12. When the Spaetzle starts to float to the surface, cover the pan and keep covered until the Spaetzle appears to swell and is fluffy. Remove the Spaetzle and repeat the cooking process with the rest of the batter.

13. When all the Spaetzle is cooked, in the Fry Pan, melt the butter over medium-high heat on the stove top. When the butter is melted, cook the Spaetzle until slightly golden.

14. To serve, divide the Spaetzle between four large plates, spoon the chicken and sauce over the Spaetzle, and serve immediately.

Chicken Scarpariello

SERVES 6

INGREDIENTS

1 3-lb chicken, cut into 8 pieces

2 ½ tsp. salt

1 ½ tsp. ground black pepper

3 tbsp. olive oil

4 sweet sausages, cut in half

6 sweet mini peppers

10 baby potatoes

1 onion, diced large

2 cloves garlic, minced

1 tbsp. balsamic vinegar

DIRECTIONS

1. Preheat the oven 400° F/204° C.

2. Season the chicken with the salt and black pepper.

3. In the High-Sided Fry Pan, heat the olive oil over medium-high heat on the stove top. When the oil is hot, brown the chicken on all sides. Remove and reserve the chicken.

4. Add the sausages and brown.

5. Add the peppers, potatoes, and onion and brown lightly.

6. Add the garlic and cook for 2 minutes.

7. Return the chicken to the pan. Transfer the pan to the oven and roast for 20–25 minutes.

8. Sprinkle the chicken with the vinegar before serving.

TIP: To cut down the preparation time of this recipe, you can use chicken breast and thighs. Cut the chicken breast in half and kick it up a notch by seasoning it with Emeril's Original Essence seasoning.

Beef, Veal, Pork & Lamb

※Pictured here

Fennel- & Shallot-Crusted Eye Round Roast

SERVES 6

INGREDIENTS

3 tbsp. olive oil

1 5-lb eye round roast, trimmed

1 tbsp. fennel seed

½ tbsp. coriander seeds

4 tsp. sea salt

2 tsp. ground black pepper

MASHED POTATOES

5 yellow potatoes, peeled

½ cup milk

1 stick butter

1 tsp. salt

½ tsp. ground black pepper

GRAVY

3 cups beef stock

3 tbsp. butter, softened

3 tbsp. flour

1 bay leaf

DIRECTIONS

1. Preheat the oven to 350° F / 177° C.

2. Use a spice mill or blender to grind the fennel seed, coriander, sea salt, and black pepper together. Rub the roast with the seasonings.

3. In the High-Sided Fry Pan, heat the olive oil over high heat on the stove top. When the oil is hot, sear the roast on all sides.

4. Transfer the pan to the oven and cook until the desired doneness is reached (about 1 hour).

5. In the Stock Pot, add the potatoes and enough water to cover the potatoes. Cover the pot with its lid. Bring to a boil on the stove top and cook the potatoes until tender.

6. Drain the potatoes and transfer to a stand mixer. Whip the potatoes with the milk, butter, salt, and black pepper. Add more milk to adjust the creaminess if necessary. Reserve the mashed potatoes in a warm place.

7. When the roast is done cooking, remove and let rest for 20 minutes before slicing.

8. Add the stock and bay leaf to the pan (do not clean out the pan). Bring the stock to a boil.

9. Combine the softened butter with the flour and whisk into the boiling beef stock. Cook until the gravy is smooth and thickened (about 10 minutes).

10. Serve the sliced roast with the Mashed Potatoes and Gravy.

Bolognese with Mezzi Rigatoni

SERVES 6

INGREDIENTS

1 lb ground beef

1 tbsp. olive oil

½ onion, chopped

3 cloves garlic, minced

1 carrot, diced small

1 cup red wine

28 oz canned crushed tomatoes

½ tbsp. sugar

1 tbsp. plus 1 tsp. salt, divided

½ tsp. ground black pepper

1 lb mezzi rigatoni

½ cup heavy cream

2 tbsp. chopped flat-leaf parsley

2 tbsp. chopped basil

grated Parmigiano-Reggiano
cheese or Romano cheese,
for serving

DIRECTIONS

1. In the High-Sided Fry Pan, heat the olive oil over high heat on the stove top. When the oil is hot, brown the meat.

2. Once the meat is browned, add the onion, garlic, and carrot. Cover the pan with its lid and cook for 3–4 minutes.

3. Add the wine and reduce by half.

4. Add the tomatoes, sugar, 1 tsp. salt, and black pepper and simmer, covered, for 30 minutes.

5. Fill the Stock Pot three quarters full with water. Add 1 tbsp. salt to the water. Bring the water to a boil on the stove top and cook the mezzi rigatoni until al dente.

6. Add the cream to the High-Sided Frying Pan and bring to a boil on the stove top.

7. Add the cooked pasta, parsley, and basil and stir to incorporate over medium heat.

8. Transfer to a pasta bowl and serve with grated cheese.

TIP: You can use almost any ground meat for this recipe instead of ground beef, including ground pork, veal, chicken, or turkey.

Rosemary- & Garlic-Crusted Pork Roast

SERVES 6

INGREDIENTS

2 white carrots, peeled & cut into 1 ½-inch pieces

2 carrots, peeled & cut into 1 ½-inch pieces

SEASONED PORK ROAST

1 3-lb pork loin

1 tbsp. plus ½ tsp. salt, divided

1 ¼ tsp. ground black pepper, divided

3 tbsp. olive oil, divided

3 tbsp. Dijon mustard

ROSEMARY-GARLIC CRUST

½ cup chopped fresh rosemary

6 garlic cloves, minced

───────────

2 tbsp. butter

½ shallot, minced

½ tsp. salt

¼ tsp. ground black pepper

DIRECTIONS

1. In the Sauce Pot, add the carrots and enough water to cover the carrots. Cover the pot with its lid. Cook for about 10 minutes over medium heat on the stove top. Drain the carrots and reserve.

2. Season the pork with 1 tbsp. salt and 1 tsp. black pepper.

3. Preheat the oven to 350° F/177° C.

4. In the High-Sided Fry Pan, heat 2 tbsp. olive oil over high heat on the stove top. When the oil is hot, sear the pork on all sides.

5. Remove the pork from the pan. Brush the pork with the mustard.

6. In a bowl, mix the rosemary and garlic with 1 tbsp. olive oil. Cover the top of the roast with the Rosemary–Garlic Crust.

7. In the High-Sided Fry Pan, melt the butter over medium-high heat on the stove top. When the butter is melted, add the shallot and carrots and brown slightly. Season with ½ tsp. salt and ¼ tsp. black pepper.

8. Add the pork to the pan. Transfer the pan to the oven and roast until an instant-read thermometer inserted into the thickest part of the pork reads 140° F/60° C.

9. Let the roast rest for 20 minutes before slicing and serving.

Spicy Pulled Pork

SERVES 6–8

INGREDIENTS

1 4-lb pork butt or pork shoulder

DRY RUB

1 tsp. ground cayenne pepper

¾ tbsp. chili powder

1 tbsp. salt

1 tsp. garlic powder

1 tsp. onion powder

SAUCE

1 cup barbeque sauce

2 tbsp. yellow mustard

2 tbsp. Worcestershire sauce

¼ cup cider vinegar

½ cup brown sugar

½ tsp. liquid smoke

DIRECTIONS

1. Preheat the oven to 325° F/163° C.

2. Combine the cayenne pepper, chili powder, salt, garlic powder, and onion powder and rub the spices into the pork.

3. Place the pork in the Stock Pot and roast, uncovered, in the oven for 2 hours.

4. In the Sauce Pot, add all the Sauce ingredients, bring to a boil on the stove top, and then turn off the heat.

5. When the pork is done, pour the Sauce over the pork. Cover the Stock Pot with its lid and return the Stock Pot to the oven. Cook until the pork is falling apart (about 1 ½ hours).

6. Serving suggestion: Use as a filling for grilled cheese, serve on hamburger rolls with red onions, or serve with macaroni and cheese.

TIP: To cook pulled pork faster, cut the pork into smaller pieces.

Roast Leg of Lamb
with Mint, Garlic & Rosemary

SERVES 2-4

INGREDIENTS

1 5-lb boneless leg of lamb

6 sprigs mint

4 cloves garlic, minced

2 tbsp. mint jelly

1 tbsp. sea salt, divided

1 ½ tsp. ground
black pepper, divided

2 tbsp. balsamic vinegar

¼ cup olive oil, divided

2 sprigs rosemary, chopped

DIRECTIONS

1. In a bowl, mix the mint, 2 cloves garlic, mint jelly, 1 tsp. salt, and ¾ tsp. black pepper. Rub the mixture on the inside of the leg of lamb. Tie the leg together with butcher's twine.

2. In a bowl, mix 2 cloves garlic, the vinegar, 2 tbsp. olive oil, rosemary, 1 tsp. salt, and ¾ tsp. black pepper. Rub the outside of the leg of lamb with the mixture. Refrigerate the leg of lamb overnight to marinate.

3. Preheat the oven to 350° F/177° C.

4. In the High-Sided Fry Pan, heat 2 tbsp. olive oil over high heat on the stove top. When the oil is hot, sear the leg of lamb on all sides.

5. Carefully transfer the pan to the oven and cook until the desired doneness is reached (about 1 ½ hours).

6. Let rest for 20 minutes before removing the twine and serving.

TIP: To add a little sweetness to this recipe, add ¼ cup currants to the inside of the roast.

Herb- & Dijon-Crusted Rack of Lamb

SERVES 2

INGREDIENTS

1 1-lb rack of lamb, cleaned

1 ½ tsp. salt

1 tsp. ground black pepper

1 tbsp. Dijon mustard

¼ cup chopped tarragon

1 sprig rosemary,
stemmed & chopped

3 sprigs thyme,
stemmed & chopped

½ cup breadcrumbs

DIRECTIONS

1. Preheat the oven 400° F/204° C.

2. Season the lamb with the salt and black pepper.

3. In the Fry Pan, heat the olive oil over high heat on the stove top. When the oil is hot, sear the lamb on all sides.

4. Brush the browned lamb with the mustard.

5. In a bowl, mix tarragon, rosemary, thyme, and breadcrumbs. Spread the seasoned breadcrumbs over the lamb.

6. Return the lamb to the Fry Pan. Roast the lamb in the oven until the desired doneness is reached. Let the lamb rest for 10 minutes before cutting and serving.

TIP: You can double this recipe by having your butcher make a crown roast of lamb instead of a rack of lamb.

Grilled Veal Chops with a Tarragon–Roasted Shallot Compound Butter

SERVES 2

INGREDIENTS

COMPOUND BUTTER

½ lb butter

3 roasted shallots

2 tsp. Creole mustard

¼ cup chopped tarragon

1 pinch salt

1 pinch ground black pepper

MARINADE

2 sprigs tarragon, chopped

1 tsp. Dijon mustard

1 shallot

3 tbsp. white balsamic vinegar

¼ cup olive oil

1 tsp. salt

½ tsp. ground black pepper

_____

2 veal rack chops, thick cut

GARLIC & OIL PASTA

1 tbsp. salt, plus more to taste

½ lb spaghetti

3 tbsp. extra virgin olive oil

2 cloves garlic, sliced

juice of ½ lemon

ground black pepper, to taste

1 tbsp. chopped flat-leaf parsley

DIRECTIONS

1. Use a food processor to pulse all the Compound Butter ingredients until mixed together. Transfer the Compound Butter to a dish and refrigerate.

2. In a shallow pan, add all the Marinade ingredients and coat the veal in the Marinade. Refrigerate for 4 hours.

3. Place the Grill Plate in the High-Sided Fry Pan. Heat the Grill Plate over medium-high heat on the stove top. When the Grill Plate is hot, grill the veal on both sides until golden and cooked (5 minutes per side). Reserve the veal.

4. Fill the Stock Pot three quarters full with water. Add 1 tbsp. salt to the water. Bring the water to a boil on the stove top. Cook the spaghetti in the boiling water until al dente.

5. In the Fry Pan, heat the extra virgin olive oil over medium heat on the stove top. When the oil is hot, cook the garlic until slightly golden.

6. Add the lemon juice and spaghetti and sauté for 2 minutes.

7. Season with the salt and black pepper and toss with the parsley.

8. Top each veal chop with 1 tbsp. Compound Butter and serve with the Garlic & Oil Pasta.

TIP: Any leftover Compound Butter can be frozen and saved for later use.

Veal Marsala with Rice Pilaf

SERVES 4

INGREDIENTS

RICE PILAF

1 tbsp. olive oil

1 tbsp. butter

½ small onion, diced

1 cup rice

1 bay leaf

1 sprig thyme

1 ¾ cups chicken stock

1 pinch salt

1 pinch ground black pepper

VEAL

1 lb veal cutlets, pounded

1 tsp. salt

½ tsp. ground black pepper

1 cup flour

3 tbsp. olive oil

3 tbsp. butter, divided

8 oz cremini mushrooms, sliced

1 shallot, minced

1 clove garlic, minced

¾ cup marsala

½ cup chicken stock

DIRECTIONS

1. In the Sauce Pot, heat 1 tbsp. olive oil and melt 1 tbsp. butter over medium heat on the stove top. When the oil is hot and the butter is melted, add the onion and sauté for 2 minutes. Add the rice and stir to coat.

2. Add the rest of the Rice Pilaf ingredients. Bring to a boil and cover the pot with its lid.

3. Reduce to a simmer and cook until all the liquid is absorbed (18–20 minutes).

4. Season the veal with 1 tsp. salt and ½ tsp. black pepper. Dredge the veal in the flour.

5. In the Fry Pan, heat 3 tbsp. olive oil over medium heat on the stove top. When the oil is hot, sear the veal on each side. Remove and reserve the veal and pour out any excess oil and flour from the pan.

6. Add 1 tbsp. butter and sauté the mushrooms for 3 minutes.

7. Add the shallot and garlic and cook for 2–3 minutes.

8. Add the marsala and stock. Reduce by half.

9. Add 2 tbsp. butter and the veal and cook until the butter is melted.

10. Serve the veal over the Rice Pilaf.

Pan-Seared Tenderloin of Beef
with Blue Cheese & Bordelaise SERVES 4

INGREDIENTS

4 8-oz filets mignon

salt, to taste

ground black pepper, to taste

3 tbsp. olive oil or grapeseed oil

1 cup crumbled blue cheese

BORDELAISE

1 large shallot, minced

1 tbsp. tomato paste

1 cup red wine

1 bay leaf

1 sprig rosemary

2 cups beef bone broth

2 tbsp. butter

salt, to taste

ground black pepper, to taste

DIRECTIONS

1. Season the filets with the salt and black pepper.

2. In the Fry Pan, heat the oil over high heat on the stove top. When the oil is hot, pan sear the filets until browned on all sides and the desired doneness is reached. Top the filets with the blue cheese. Reserve the filets and keep warm.

3. Add the shallot to the pan and sauté for 2 minutes.

4. Add the tomato paste and sauté for 2 minutes.

5. Add the red wine, bay leaf, and rosemary and reduce by two thirds.

6. Add the broth and reduce by half.

7. Add the butter, season with the salt and pepper, and cook for 3–4 minutes.

8. Pour the Bordelaise over the filets before serving.

TIP: Garnish with fried shallots: Slice 2 shallots into eighths, place in a cup of milk, dredge in flour, and fry with oil in the High-Sided Fry Pan over high heat until crispy. Drain on paper towels and top the filets before serving.

Skirt Steak with Creole-Seasoned Compound Butter

SERVES 4

INGREDIENTS

1 1 ½-lb skirt steak, trimmed

MARINADE

1 shallot

3 tbsp. balsamic vinegar

¼ cup olive oil

1 tsp. salt

½ tsp. coarsely ground black pepper

COMPOUND BUTTER

½ lb butter

2 tbsp. Creole mustard

3 scallions, chopped

4 cloves garlic, roasted

2 tbsp. chopped cilantro

DIRECTIONS

1. IIn a shallow pan, mix all the Marinade ingredients. Coat the skirt steak in the marinade and refrigerate for 4 hours.

2. When the steak is done marinating, pulse all the Compound Butter ingredients in a food processor until blended. Refrigerate the Compound Butter until ready to use.

3. Place the Grill Plate in the High-Sided Fry Pan. Heat the Grill Plate over high heat on the stove top. When the Grill Plate is hot, remove the steak from the marinade and grill until the desired doneness is reached.

4. Slice and serve the steak topped with the Compound Butter.

TIP: This recipe also works great with other steaks, including flank or hanger steak.

Steak Diane

SERVES 2

INGREDIENTS

2 12-oz New York strip steaks

1 tsp. salt

½ tsp. ground black pepper

1 tbsp. olive oil

SAUCE

1 shallot, minced

1 tbsp. Dijon mustard

1 tbsp. Worcestershire sauce

¼ cup brandy or cognac

½ cup beef stock

¼ cup heavy cream

2 tbsp. butter

salt, to taste

ground black pepper, to taste

DIRECTIONS

1. Season the steaks on both sides with the salt and black pepper.

2. In the Fry Pan, heat the olive oil over high heat on the stove top. When the oil is hot, sear the steaks on both sides and cook until the desired doneness is reached. Reserve the steaks on a plate.

3. Add the shallot and cook for 1 minute.

4. Add the mustard and Worcestershire sauce and stir. Add the brandy, stock, and any juice from the plate with the steaks and reduce by two thirds.

5. Add the cream and butter and cook for 2 minutes.

6. Season with salt and black pepper.

7. Turn off the heat. Return the steaks to the Fry Pan and coat with the Sauce.

8. Serve the steaks with the Sauce.

TIP: To add a little extra "heat" to your steak, crust the steak with black cracked peppercorns before searing.

Pan-Seared Pork Medallions
with Dried Apricot Sauce SERVES 4

INGREDIENTS

PORK MEDALLIONS

8 pork medallions,
pounded slightly

salt, to taste

ground black pepper, to taste

3 tbsp. olive oil

DRIED APRICOT SAUCE

1 shallot, minced

½ cup diced dried apricots
(or 4 fresh apricots, diced)

½ cup Riesling wine

1 sprig sage

2 cups chicken stock

3 tbsp. butter

DIRECTIONS

1. Season the pork with the salt and black pepper.

2. In the High-Sided Fry Pan, heat the olive oil over high heat on the stove top. When the oil is hot, pan sear the pork on both sides. Remove and reserve the pork.

3. Add the shallot and apricots and sauté for about 2 minutes.

4. Add the wine and sage and reduce by half.

5. Add the stock and reduce by about half.

6. Add the butter.

7. Serve the pork with the Dried Apricot Sauce.

TIP: Try using chicken instead of pork for a new twist on this recipe.

Beef Braciola

SERVES 8

INGREDIENTS

1 2 ½-lb top round London broil

4 cloves garlic, minced

½ cup basil pesto

½ cup shredded Romano cheese

½ cup raisins, soaked in warm water

¼ cup pine nuts, toasted

salt, to taste

ground black pepper, to taste

2 tbsp. olive oil

SAUCE

1 small onion, diced small

3 cloves garlic, minced

1 ½ cups red wine

28 oz canned crushed tomatoes

1 tsp. salt

1 tbsp. sugar

¼ cup chopped flat-leaf parsley

CREAMY POLENTA

3 cups chicken stock

½ cup heavy cream

1 sprig rosemary

1 cup polenta

3 tbsp. butter, divided

½ cup freshly grated Parmigiano-Reggiano cheese

1 tsp. salt

¼ tsp. ground black pepper

DIRECTIONS

1. Cut the London broil in half in the middle. Slice the halves horizontally into four equal slices (eight slices total) and pound thin with a meat mallet.

2. Place a small sprinkle of garlic on each meat slice. Spread 1 tbsp. pesto, 1 tbsp. Romano, 1 tbsp. raisins, and 1 tsp. pine nuts (in order) on each meat slice. Roll and tie each end with butcher's twine. Season each braciola with the salt and black pepper.

3. In the Stock Pot, heat the olive oil over high heat on the stove top. When the oil is hot, sear the braciola on all sides until browned. Remove and reserve the braciola.

4. Add the onion and garlic and sauté over medium heat for about 3 minutes.

5. Add the wine and braciola. Cover with the crushed tomatoes. Add the sugar and salt. Cover the pot with its lid and simmer over low heat for 2 hours.

6. When the braciola is almost done, make the Creamy Polenta: In the Sauce Pot, bring the stock, cream, and rosemary to a boil. Slowly whisk the polenta into the mixture and cook until thick and creamy. Add the butter and cheese and stir until incorporated and the butter has melted. Season the Creamy Polenta with the salt and black pepper.

7. Remove the braciola and remove the twine. Add the parsley to the Sauce. Slice the braciola and serve with the Creamy Polenta and Sauce.

Pot Roast
with Rosemary Brown Sauce SERVES 4

INGREDIENTS

1 3 ½-lb chuck roast

¾ tsp. salt

1 tsp. ground black pepper

3 tbsp. olive oil

1 small onion, diced small

1 carrot, diced small

1 stalk celery, diced small

2 cloves garlic, minced

1 shallot, minced

2 tbsp. tomato paste

1 cup red wine

3 cups beef stock

1 sprig rosemary

2 sprigs thyme

1 bay leaf

mashed potatoes or creamy polenta, for serving

DIRECTIONS

1. Season the roast generously on all sides with the salt and black pepper.

2. In the Stock Pot, heat the olive oil over high heat on the stove top. When the oil is hot, brown the roast well on all sides. Remove and reserve the roast.

3. Add the onion, carrot, celery, garlic, and shallot to the pan, lower the heat to medium, and cook until slightly browned.

4. Preheat the oven 375° F/191° C.

5. Add the tomato paste, stir, and cook for about 1 minute.

6. Add the wine, stock, roast, rosemary, thyme, and bay leaf, cover the pot with its lid, and bring to a boil.

7. Transfer the pot to the oven and cook until tender (2 hours). Transfer the roast to a carving board and cover lightly with foil.

8. Bring the sauce to a gentle simmer over medium-high heat and reduce to the desired thickness.

9. Serving suggestion: Slice the pot roast and serve over mashed potatoes or creamy polenta with the sauce.

Pork Osso Bucco

SERVES 4

INGREDIENTS

PORK SHANKS

4 12-oz pork shanks

1 tbsp. sea salt

1 tbsp. ground black pepper

3 tbsp. olive oil

VEGETABLES

1 shallot, minced

2 cloves garlic, minced

1 onion, diced small

2 carrots, diced small

2 stalks celery, diced small

2 tbsp. tomato paste

2 cups white wine

2 cups beef stock

1 bay leaf

2 sprigs oregano

3 tbsp. chopped parsley

mashed potatoes, for serving

DIRECTIONS

1. Season the pork shanks with the salt and black pepper.

2. In the Stock Pot, heat the olive oil over high heat on the stove top. When the oil is hot, brown the pork shanks. Then, remove and reserve the pork shanks.

3. Preheat the oven to 400° F/204° C.

4. Add the shallot, garlic, onion, carrots, and celery to the Stock Pot and cook over medium heat for 4 minutes.

5. Add the tomato paste and stir to combine.

6. Add the pork shanks, wine, stock, bay leaf, oregano, and parsley and bring to a boil.

7. Cover the pot with its lid and transfer the pot to the oven. Cook until the meat is tender and falling off the bone (about 2 ½ hours). When the pork shanks are done cooking, remove and reserve them.

8. Transfer the Stock Pot back to the stove top and reduce the liquid until slightly thickened to make a sauce.

9. Serve the pork shanks with the sauce, vegetables, and mashed potatoes.

Seafood

⁂Pictured here

Pan-Fried Breaded Flounder

SERVES 2

INGREDIENTS

2 large eggs

2 tbsp. milk

1 cup flour

2 3–4-oz pieces flounder

1 cup breadcrumbs

1 cup panko breadcrumbs

1 tsp. granulated onion

1 tsp. granulated garlic

1 tsp. salt

½ tsp. ground black pepper

GREENS

1 cup microgreens

1 cup arugula

juice of ½ lemon

2 tbsp. extra virgin olive oil

salt, to taste

ground black pepper, to taste

---

1 cup large cherry tomatoes, quartered

1 tsp. extra virgin olive oil

½ lemon, cut into wedges, for garnish

DIRECTIONS

1. In a bowl, beat the eggs with the milk.

2. In a shallow pan, add the flour.

3. In a separate pan, combine the breadcrumbs, panko breadcrumbs, onion, garlic, salt, and black pepper.

4. Dredge the flounder in the flour, then the eggs, and finally the breadcrumbs.

5. In the High-Sided Fry Pan, heat about 2 inches of canola oil over medium heat on the stove top. When the oil is hot, sauté the flounder on each side until lightly golden and cooked through. Transfer to the Crisper to drain briefly before serving.

6. In a bowl, add the microgreens and arugula. Squeeze the lemon half over the greens and toss with 2 tbsp. extra virgin olive oil and the salt and black pepper.

7. Serve the flounder on two plates and serve with the greens and tomatoes. Drizzle 1 tsp. extra virgin olive oil over the tomatoes and garnish with the lemon wedges.

TIP: To make this recipe keto friendly, use ground-up nuts (like almonds) for the crust instead of the breadcrumbs and flour.

Emeril's Essence-Crusted
Tuna with a Mango Salsa

SERVES 2

INGREDIENTS

MANGO SALSA

1 mango, peeled & diced

½ red bell pepper, diced

2 tbsp. chopped cilantro

¼ red onion, diced

½ jalapeño, minced

juice of ½ lime

1 pinch salt

WASABI AIOLI

2 tbsp. wasabi paste

½ cup mayonnaise

_____

2 10-oz tuna steaks

2 tbsp. Emeril's Original
Essence seasoning

2 tbsp. grapeseed oil

DIRECTIONS

1. In a bowl, combine the Mango Salsa ingredients. Reserve the Mango Salsa.

2. In a separate bowl, combine the Wasabi Aioli ingredients. Reserve the Wasabi Aioli.

3. Coat the tuna steaks in the Essence seasoning.

4. In the High-Sided Fry Pan, heat the grapeseed oil over high heat on the stove top. When the oil is hot, sear the tuna to the desired doneness.

5. Slice the tuna and serve with the Mango Salsa and Wasabi Aioli.

TIP: To mix things up, add black beans to the salsa.

Sole Almondine

SERVES 4

INGREDIENTS

2 large eggs

3 tbsp. milk

1 tsp. salt

½ tsp. ground black pepper

2 cups flour

3 tbsp. olive oil

4 3-oz sole fillets

SAUCE

1 shallot, minced

¼ cup butter

¼ cup sliced almonds, toasted

⅓ cup white wine

juice of ½ lemon

½ tsp. ground black pepper

salt, to taste

ground black pepper, to taste

1 tbsp. parsley, for garnish

DIRECTIONS

1. In a bowl, beat the eggs with the milk, salt, and black pepper.

2. In a shallow pan, add the flour.

3. Dredge the sole in the flour and then dip in the eggs.

4. In the High-Sided Fry Pan, heat the olive oil over medium-high heat on the stove top. When the oil is hot, fry the sole in two batches. Fry each side for 3 minutes. Remove and reserve on a platter.

5. Clean out the pan. Add the shallot, butter, almonds, wine, and lemon juice. Reduce over medium-high heat on the stove top until slightly thickened. Taste the sauce and season with the salt and black pepper.

6. Pour the sauce over the sole and garnish with the parsley before serving.

TIP: If you can't find sole for this recipe, you can use cod or flounder instead.

Blackened Salmon Tostados

MAKES 12

INGREDIENTS

TORTILLAS

canola oil, for frying

12 6-inch corn tortillas

SALMON

1 lb salmon

1 ½ tbsp. Emeril's Original Essence seasoning

½ tsp. ground cayenne pepper

2 tbsp. olive oil

_____

2 cups shredded red cabbage

PINEAPPLE SALSA

2 cups small-diced pineapple

½ jalapeño, minced

2 tbsp. chopped cilantro

2 scallions, chopped

juice of ½ lime

½ red bell pepper, diced small

LIME AIOLI

½ cup mayonnaise

juice & zest of 1 lime

DIRECTIONS

1. In the High-Sided Fry Pan, heat about 2 inches of canola oil over medium-high heat on the stove top. When the oil reaches 375° F/191° C, fry the tortillas until crispy. Transfer to the Crisper to drain briefly before serving.

2. In a bowl, combine the Essence seasoning and cayenne pepper. Season the salmon evenly with the spices.

3. Heat the Fry Pan over high heat on the stove top. When the pan is hot, place the salmon, meat side down, in the pan. Pour the olive oil over the salmon and cook until blackened. Flip and cook until the fish is almost done. Then, turn the heat off.

4. In a bowl, combine the Pineapple Salsa ingredients.

5. Break the salmon up into pieces. Place the crispy tortillas on a work surface. Top with some red cabbage, Pineapple Salsa, and pieces of salmon and repeat until all the ingredients are used up.

6. In a bowl, combine the Lime Aioli ingredients.

7. Serve the salmon tostados with the Lime Aioli.

TIP: To make this recipe keto friendly, use iceburg lettuce instead of the tortillas.

Pan-Seared Scallops over Risotto

SERVES 2

INGREDIENTS

RISOTTO

2 tbsp. olive oil

2 tbsp. butter, divided

½ onion, diced small

1 shallot, minced

⅔ cup Arborio rice

½ cup white wine

1 sprig fresh thyme

1 bay leaf

½ tsp. salt, plus more to taste

¼ tsp. ground black pepper, plus more to taste

3 cups chicken stock

¼ cup Parmigiano-Reggiano cheese

SCALLOPS

3 tbsp. olive oil

¾ lb large dry sea scallops

salt, to taste

ground black pepper, to taste

SAUCE

2 tbsp. pine nuts

juice of 1 lemon

¼ cup plus 1 tbsp. butter

¼ cup white wine

salt, to taste

ground black pepper, to taste

DIRECTIONS

1. In the Sauce Pot, heat 2 tbsp. olive oil and melt 1 tbsp. butter over medium heat on the stove top. When the oil is hot and the butter is melted, add the onion and shallot and cook for 1 minute.

2. Add the rice and coat well. Add ½ cup wine and let it absorb into the risotto. Add the thyme, bay leaf, salt, black pepper, and 1 cup stock and stir until all the stock is absorbed. Continue adding 1 cup stock at a time and stirring until all the stock is used. The rice is done when it is tender but still al dente. Add the cheese and 1 tbsp. butter and stir. Season with additional salt and black pepper if necessary.

3. In the Fry Pan, heat 3 tbsp. olive oil over high heat on the stove top. Season the scallops with the salt and black pepper. When the oil is hot, sauté the scallops until done. Reserve and keep warm.

4. In the Fry Pan, add the pine nuts and toast slightly over medium-high heat on the stove top.

5. Add the lemon juice, butter, and ¼ cup wine and reduce.

6. Serve the scallops with the risotto and top with the sauce.

Shrimp, Lobster & Scallop with
Spinach Linguine in a Sherry Cream Sauce SERVES 4

INGREDIENTS

SPINACH LINGUINE

½ tsp. salt

12 oz spinach linguine

SEAFOOD

2 tbsp. olive oil

4 4-oz lobster tails

8 16–20-size shrimp, peeled & deveined

8 large sea scallops

_____

2 shallots, minced

2 plum tomatoes, diced

1 cup white wine

1 ½ cups chicken, vegetable, or shrimp stock

6 sprigs tarragon, chopped

1 ½ cups heavy cream

½ tsp. salt

¼ tsp. ground black pepper

½ cup sherry

DIRECTIONS

1. Fill the Stock Pot with water, bring to a boil, and add 2 tbsp. salt. Cook the spinach linguine until al dente.

2. In the High-Sided Fry Pan, heat the olive oil over high heat on the stove top. When the oil is hot, sear the lobster tails, shrimp, and scallops. Remove the seafood from the pan and reserve.

3. Add the shallots and sauté for 2 minutes.

4. Add the diced tomatoes, wine, and stock and reduce by half.

5. Add the cream, tarragon, salt, and black pepper and bring to a boil for 3 minutes.

6. Add the sherry, seafood, and linguine and toss. Bring to a boil.

7. Remove and serve.

TIP: If you can't find shrimp stock for this recipe, use shrimp base and follow the directions on the label to make stock.

Fish & Chips
with Tartar Sauce & Coleslaw

SERVES 4

INGREDIENTS

TARTAR SAUCE

1 cup mayonnaise

3 tbsp. dill pickle relish

1 pinch ground
cayenne pepper

½ shallot, minced

juice of 1 lemon wedge

1 tbsp. chopped parsley

COLESLAW

½ head cabbage, shredded

1 tbsp. red onion, minced

1 carrot, shredded

⅓ cup mayonnaise

2 tbsp. pineapple juice

juice of ¼ lemon

½ red pepper, diced small

1 pinch salt

1 pinch ground black pepper

BEER-BATTERED FISH

12 oz beer

2 large eggs

3 cups flour, divided

1 tsp. baking powder

½ tsp. salt

¼ tsp. ground black pepper

1 tsp. Emeril's Original
Essence seasoning

4 5-oz white fish fillets (scrod,
haddock, grouper, or catfish)

10 cups vegetable oil, for frying

CHIPS

2 lb white potatoes, peeled &
cut into ¼ inch-thick chips

salt, to taste

ground black pepper, to taste

_____

¼ cup malt vinegar, for serving
with the chips

DIRECTIONS

1. In a bowl, combine the Tartar Sauce ingredients.

2. In a large bowl, combine the Coleslaw ingredients until well mixed.

3. In a medium-size bowl, whisk together the beer, eggs, 2 ½ cups flour, baking powder, salt, and black pepper until thick, frothy, and thoroughly blended.

4. In a separate bowl, combine ½ cup flour with the Essence seasoning.

5. In the Stock Pot, heat the vegetable oil to 365° F/185° C. When the oil is hot, fry the potatoes in two batches (3 minutes per batch) to make the Chips. Remove and drain on paper towels for 2 minutes. Return the Chips to the Stock Pot and continue to fry until golden brown (3–5 minutes). Remove, drain on a paper towel-lined plate, and season with salt and black pepper before serving. Keep the Chips warm.

6. Cut each fillet in half crosswise. Dredge the fillets in the seasoned flour and then the batter. Fry the fish in the oil. Turn each piece once or twice and cook until the fillets are puffed, crispy, and golden brown (about 7–10 minutes; cook in batches if necessary. Transfer to the Crisper with paper towels to drain briefly. Then, keep each batch warm in the oven while you finish the other batches and the chips).

7. For each serving, serve two fillet halves with the Chips, malt vinegar, some Coleslaw, and a few spoonfuls of the Tartar Sauce.

Shrimp & Grits

SERVES 4

INGREDIENTS

¼ cup olive oil, divided

½ lb Andouille sausage, sliced

2 cloves garlic, minced

1 small onion, sliced

1 green pepper, sliced

1 cup shrimp, chicken, or
vegetable stock

2 ⅓ tbsp. Emeril's Original
Essence seasoning, divided

1 tsp. ground cayenne pepper

1 lb 16–20-size shrimp,
cleaned & deveined

GRITS

1 ½ cups instant grits

¼ cup heavy cream

2 tbsp. butter

¾ cup shredded cheddar

salt, to taste

ground black pepper, to taste

DIRECTIONS

1. In the High-Sided Fry Pan, heat 2 tbsp. olive oil over medium-high heat on the stove top. When the oil is hot, brown the sausage.

2. Add the garlic, onion, and pepper and cook until slightly tender (4–5 minutes).

3. Add the stock and 1 tsp. Essence seasoning and cook for about 5 minutes. Reserve.

4. In a small bowl, mix the cayenne pepper and 2 tbsp. Essence seasoning. Sprinkle both sides of the shrimp with the seasoning mixture.

5. In the Fry Pan, heat 2 tbsp. olive oil over high heat on the stove top. When the oil is hot, sear the shrimp on both sides.

6. Turn the heat off and add some of the liquid from the High-Sided Fry Pan to the Fry Pan to deglaze. Pour the shrimp into the High-Sided Fry Pan and cook over high heat on the stove top until done.

7. In the Sauce Pot, prepare the grits according to the instructions on the packaging.

8. Mix in the heavy cream, butter, and cheddar and season with the salt and black pepper.

9. Serve the shrimp and sausage over the grits.

TIP: To make this recipe meatless, use plant-based hot sausage instead of Andouille.

Shrimp Francaise

SERVES 2

INGREDIENTS

1 cup flour

2 large eggs

1 tsp. salt

½ tsp. ground black pepper

1 tbsp. chopped parsley

⅓ cup olive oil

½ lb 16–20-size shrimp, peeled & deveined

SAUCE

1 cup chicken or shrimp stock

1 cup white wine

juice of 1 lemon

¼ cup butter

2 tbsp. capers

salt, to taste

ground black pepper, to taste

ZUCCHINI & YELLOW SQUASH SPAGHETTI

3 tbsp. extra virgin olive oil

2 cloves garlic, sliced

1 zucchini, spiralized

1 yellow squash, spiralized

½ red bell pepper, sliced small

Louisiana hot sauce, for serving

DIRECTIONS

1. In a shallow pan, add the flour.

2. In a bowl, beat the eggs with the salt, black pepper, and parsley.

3. In the High-Sided Fry Pan, heat the olive oil over medium-high heat on the stove top. Dip the shrimp into the flour and then the eggs. When the oil is hot, fry the shrimp until slightly browned. Remove and reserve the shrimp and remove any excess oil from the pan.

4. In the High-Sided Fry Pan, add the stock and wine and reduce by half.

5. Add the lemon juice and butter and cook until the butter is melted and creamy.

6. Add the shrimp and capers and season with the salt and black pepper.

7. In the Fry Pan, heat the extra virgin olive oil over high heat on the stove top. When the oil is hot, sauté the garlic, zucchini, squash, and red pepper until al dente.

8. Serve the spaghetti with the shrimp and sauce.

TIP: You can also make this recipe with cod instead of shrimp by cutting the cod into three pieces.

Portuguese Clam Bake

SERVES 4

INGREDIENTS

4 boneless & skinless chicken thighs

1 tbsp. Emeril's Original Essence seasoning

2 tbsp. olive oil

½ lb chorizo sausage, sliced

12 oz beer

8 baby red potatoes

2 bay leaves

24 littleneck clams

½ stick butter

2 ears sweet corn, shucked & broken into smaller pieces

3 tbsp. chopped parsley, for garnish

crusty bread, for serving

DIRECTIONS

1. Season the chicken thighs with the Essence seasoning.

2. In the Fry Pan, heat the olive oil over high heat on the stove top. When the oil is hot, sauté the chicken thighs on both sides and brown the chorizo.

3. Deglaze the pan with one quarter of the beer and pour into the Stock Pot.

4. Add the potatoes, bay leaves, and the rest of the beer to the Stock Pot and simmer with the pan covered for about 20 minutes.

5. Add the clams, butter, and corn and boil with the pan covered until the clams open. Discard any unopened clams.

6. Top with the parsley before serving. Serve in shallow bowls with crusty bread on the side.

TIP: To kick this recipe up a notch, you can add lobster tails to the pot too.

Soups, Stews & One-Pot Meals

※Pictured here

Tomato & Fennel Soup with Grilled Cheese

SERVES 6

INGREDIENTS

TOMATO & FENNEL SOUP

1 onion, sliced

1 large fennel bulb, sliced

1 shallot, minced

3 tbsp. olive oil

5 tomatoes, quartered

3 tbsp. tomato paste

1 qt. vegetable or chicken broth

½ cup heavy cream

1 bay leaf

salt, to taste

ground black pepper, to taste

GRILLED CHEESE

8 slices bread

½ cup butter, softened

12 slices cheddar cheese

DIRECTIONS

1. In the Stock Pot, cook the onion, fennel, and shallot in the olive oil over medium heat on the stove top until tender (about 10 minutes).

2. Add the tomatoes, cover the pot with its lid, and cook for about 5 minutes.

3. Add the broth and bay leaf (keep the lid on the pot), bring to a boil, and then reduce to a simmer for 20 minutes.

4. Remove the bay leaf and use an immersion blender to blend the soup. Add the cream, salt, and black pepper and keep warm.

5. Heat the Fry Pan over medium heat on the stove top. Butter one side of each bread slice. When the Fry Pan is hot, place four bread slices, buttered side down, in the Fry Pan. Top each bread slice in the pan with three cheddar slices. Top with the rest of the bread slices, buttered sides up. Fry the sandwiches on both sides until golden and the cheese is melted.

6. Cut the sandwiches in half and serve with the soup.

TIP: The riper the tomato, the sweeter the soup, so the best time of year to make this recipe is summer.

New England Clam Chowder

SERVES 6

INGREDIENTS

6 oz salt pork, diced

1 onion, diced

2 stalks celery, diced

½ green pepper, diced

1 shallot, minced

¼ cup plus 1 tbsp. butter

¼ cup plus 1 tbsp. flour

1 ½ qt. clam broth

1 sprig thyme

1 bay leaf

3 yellow potatoes, diced

1 cup heavy cream

3 cups chopped clams, raw

ground black pepper, to taste

parsley, chopped, for serving

DIRECTIONS

1. In the Stock Pot, cook the salt pork over medium heat until crispy.

2. Add the onion, celery, green pepper, and shallot and cook until tender.

3. Add the butter and melt. When the butter is melted, add the flour and cook for 4 minutes while stirring.

4. Use a whisk to add the clam broth slowly until creamy.

5. Add the thyme and bay leaf. Simmer for 20 minutes.

6. Add the potatoes and simmer until the potatoes are tender (about 15 minutes).

7. Add the cream and simmer for 5 minutes.

8. Add the clams, remove from the heat, and season with the black pepper. Remove and discard the thyme sprig and bay leaf. Serve the chowder in bowls garnished with the chopped parsley.

TIP: You can use cherrystone clams in this recipe. Just steam until they open slightly, let cool, and chop. Strain the liquid in the pot and use the liquid as part of the broth.

Turkey Andouille Gumbo

SERVES 6

INGREDIENTS

GUMBO

1 ½ cups canola or vegetable oil

1 ½ cups flour

1 cup chopped onions

½ cup chopped green
bell pepper

½ cup chopped celery

1 tbsp. minced garlic

2 cups sliced Andouille sausage

2 qt. turkey stock

2 bay leaves

2 tsp. salt, plus more to taste

ground cayenne pepper,
to taste

1 tsp. Emeril's Original
Essence seasoning

2 cups cooked & shredded
turkey meat

RICE

1 cup long-grain white rice

2 cups water

2 tbsp. butter

½ tsp. salt

_____

steamed rice, for serving

chopped scallions, for garnish

DIRECTIONS

1. In the Stock Pot, slowly heat the oil and flour together over low heat on the stove top while stirring constantly until the mixture turns a nutty brown color and is very fragrant (be careful not to burn).

2. Add the onions, green pepper, and celery and cook while stirring for 4 minutes.

3. Add the garlic and sausage and cook until some fat releases from the sausage (about 5 minutes).

4. Add the stock, bay leaves, 2 tsp. salt, cayenne pepper, and Essence seasoning. Bring to a boil and then reduce the heat and simmer for 1 hour. If the gumbo gets too thick, it can be thinned by adding a bit of additional water or stock.

5. Add the turkey and simmer for 30 minutes.

6. When the Gumbo is 20 minutes from being ready, make the Rice: In the Sauce Pot, add the rice, water, butter, and salt and bring to a boil on the stove top. Reduce to a simmer and cook, covered, for 18 minutes.

7. When the Gumbo is ready, adjust the seasoning and serve in bowls over hot steamed rice, garnished with a generous sprinkle of scallions.

Creamy Potato Leek Soup

SERVES 6

INGREDIENTS

½ stick butter

1 bunch leeks,
cleaned well & chopped

1 shallot, minced

2 cloves garlic, minced

5 large Yukon Gold potatoes,
peeled & cut in half

1 ½ qt. chicken stock

1 bay leaf

1 sprig rosemary

1 cup heavy cream

salt, to taste

ground black pepper, to taste

DIRECTIONS

1. In the Stock Pot, melt the butter over medium heat on the stove top. When the butter is melted, sauté the leeks, shallot, and garlic until tender.

2. Add the potatoes, stock, bay leaf, and rosemary and simmer until the potatoes are tender (30–40 minutes).

3. Remove the bay leaf and rosemary. Add the cream and cook for 3 minutes.

4. Turn off the heat. Use an immersion blender to blend the soup until creamy.

5. Season with the salt and black pepper before serving.

TIP: If you have leftover mashed potatoes, you can use them in this recipe. Just add the mashed potatoes after you add the liquid. You will need about 3 cups of mashed potatoes for this recipe.

Chicken & Dumplings

SERVES 6

INGREDIENTS

1 5-lb chicken

2 qt. unsalted chicken broth

2 sprigs thyme

1 bay leaf

_____

SAUCE

¼ cup butter

1 onion, diced

3 stalks celery, diced

3 carrots, diced

1 shallot, minced

¼ cup flour

½ cup heavy cream

salt, to taste

ground black pepper

DUMPLINGS

2 ¼ cups flour

2 tbsp. sugar

½ cup butter

1 tbsp. baking powder

½ tsp. salt

½ tsp. cream of tartar

1 large egg

¾ cup milk

DIRECTIONS

1. In the Stock Pot, simmer the chicken with the broth, thyme, and bay leaf on the stove top, covered, for 1 hour.

2. When the chicken is done simmering, remove and cool so that you can remove the meat from the bones. Strain the broth and reserve. Clean out the Stock Pot.

3. In the Stock Pot, add the butter, onion, celery, carrots, and shallot and sweat until translucent.

4. Add the flour and stir with a wooden spoon. Cook over low heat for about 5 minutes, stirring a few times.

5. Whisk one third of the stock into the pot at a time, whisking until the sauce looks creamy. Simmer for 30 minutes.

6. Remove the chicken from the bone and add to the simmering sauce. Add the cream and stir. Season with the salt and black pepper.

7. To make the Dumplings: In a bowl, combine the flour, sugar, butter, baking powder, salt, and cream of tartar. Use a fork to cut the butter into the dough. In a separate bowl, beat the egg and milk. Add to the dough and mix until combined.

8. Use an ice cream scoop to drop the dumplings into the simmering sauce. Cover the pot with its lid and simmer until the Dumplings are cooked through (about 20 minutes).

Braised Beef Pappardelle
Drizzled with Truffle Oil

SERVES 6

INGREDIENTS

2 tbsp. olive oil

1 ½ cups sliced shiitake mushrooms

2 cloves garlic, minced

1 shallot, minced

1 ½ cups braised beef (see Pot Roast with Rosemary Brown Sauce)

1 cup beef stock

½ cup red wine

1 tbsp. salt

1 lb pappardelle

3 tbsp. butter

1 tbsp. truffle oil

¼ cup chopped Italian parsley

ground black pepper, to taste

grated Parmesan or Romano cheese, for serving

DIRECTIONS

1. In the High-Sided Fry Pan, heat the olive oil over high heat on the stove top. When the oil is hot, sauté the mushrooms, garlic, and shallot.

2. Add the beef, stock, and wine and reduce by half.

3. Fill the Stock Pot three quarters full with water, add the salt, and bring to a boil on the stove top. When the water is boiling, add the pappardelle and cook until al dente.

4. Toss the cooked pappardelle with the braised beef. Add the butter and cook until the butter is melted.

5. Place the pasta in a pasta bowl and drizzle with the truffle oil. Sprinkle with the parsley and serve garnished with the black pepper and cheese.

TIP: This recipe also great with pork. If you have leftover pork from the Spicy Pulled Pork recipe, use the leftover pork instead of the beef.

Pasta with Chicken & Peas

SERVES 4-6

INGREDIENTS

PASTA

1 tbsp. salt

1 lb farfalle

_____

1 tbsp. olive oil

2 oz pancetta, chopped

2 chicken breasts, diced

½ shallot, minced

2 cloves garlic, minced

1 cup chicken stock or broth

1 cup heavy cream

1 cup petite peas, frozen or fresh

salt, to taste

ground black pepper, to taste

grated Parmesan cheese,
for serving

DIRECTIONS

1. Fill the Stock Pot three quarters full with water, add the salt, and bring to a boil on the stove top. Cook the pasta in the Stock Pot until al dente.

2. While the water comes to a boil, prepare the rest of the dish: In the High-Sided Fry Pan, heat the olive oil over high heat on the stove top. When the oil is hot, add the pancetta and cook until crispy.

3. Add the chicken and brown lightly.

4. Add the shallots and garlic and cook until the garlic is slightly golden (about 2 minutes).

5. Add the stock and cream to the High-Sided Fry Pan and reduce by half.

6. Add the peas and cook for 1 minute.

7. Add the hot pasta, toss, and cook for 1 minute. Season with the salt and black pepper.

8. Serve garnished with the cheese.

TIP: You can make this same recipe with shrimp instead of chicken: Pan sear the shrimp on both sides and then reserve the shrimp. Add the shrimp back to the pan once you add the pasta and toss a few times until the shrimp and pasta are fully cooked and the cream thickens slightly.

Beef Stew

SERVES 4-6

INGREDIENTS

2 lb beef chuck, cubed

1 tbsp. Emeril's Original Essence seasoning

¼ cup flour

2 tbsp. olive oil

1 cup pearl onions, peeled

4 carrots, peeled & cut into large chunks

4 cloves garlic, minced

2 tbsp. tomato paste

2 cups red wine

1 lb baby potatoes

2 tbsp. balsamic vinegar

3 cups beef stock

1 bay leaf

3 sprigs thyme

DIRECTIONS

1. Season the beef with the Essence seasoning and coat with the flour.

2. In the Stock Pot, heat the olive oil over high heat on the stove top. When the oil is hot, brown the beef. Remove and reserve the beef.

3. Add the onions, carrots, and garlic and cook for 2 minutes.

4. Add the tomato paste and cook for 1 minute.

5. Add the beef and wine and reduce the wine by half.

6. Add the rest of the ingredients, stir, and cover the pot with its lid. Lower the heat and simmer until the meat is tender (1 ½–2 hours).

7. Season with the salt and black pepper before serving.

TIP: Instead of beef stew, you can also follow this recipe to make lamb or venison stew. You can also use beer instead of the wine.

Braised Chicken Thighs with Hot Sausage, Plum Tomatoes & Potatoes

SERVES 4

INGREDIENTS

6 bone-in chicken thighs

1 tsp. salt

1 tsp. ground black pepper

2 tbsp. olive oil

6 hot sausage links, cut into half

1 small onion, diced

3 cloves garlic, minced

4 medium-size red potatoes, quartered

28 oz canned plum tomatoes

1 sprig thyme

1 bay leaf

crusty bread, for serving

DIRECTIONS

1. Preheat the oven 350° F/177° C.

2. Season the chicken with the salt and black pepper.

3. In the Stock Pot, heat the olive oil over high heat on the stove top. When the oil is hot, brown the chicken on both sides. Remove and reserve the chicken.

4. Add the sausage and cook until browned.

5. Add the onion and garlic and sauté for 3 minutes.

6. Add the chicken, potatoes, tomatoes, thyme, and bay leaf.

7. Cover the pot with its lid. Transfer the pot to the oven and cook until the potatoes are tender and the chicken is fall-off-the-bone tender (30–40 minutes).

8. Serve with crusty bread.

TIP: To cut down this recipe's cooking time, you can use boneless chicken thighs. You can also use any flavor of sausage instead of the hot sausage to suit your tastes.

Portuguese Soup

SERVES 6

INGREDIENTS

3 tbsp. olive oil

1 onion, diced

3 celery stalks, diced

3 carrots, diced

4 cloves garlic, minced

1 lb linguiça, sliced ¼ inch thick

1 tsp. smoked paprika

28 oz canned plum tomatoes

15 oz canned cannellini beans, drained

6 cups chicken broth

4 potatoes, diced

4 cups chopped kale

1 bay leaf

salt, to taste

ground black pepper, to taste

chopped parsley, for garnish

DIRECTIONS

1. In the Stock Pot, heat the olive oil over medium heat on the stove top. When the oil is hot, sauté the onion, celery, carrots, garlic, and linguiça for 4–5 minutes.

2. Add the paprika and cook for 1 minute.

3. Squeeze the tomatoes to break them up slightly. Add the tomatoes, beans, broth, potatoes, kale, and bay leaf. Cover the pot with its lid and simmer for 30 minutes.

4. Season with the salt and black pepper before serving. Garnish with the parsley.

TIP: To make this soup vegetarian, remove the linguiça and use vegetable stock.

Country-Style Pork & Chicken Cassoulet

SERVES 6

INGREDIENTS

1 ham hock

1 lb dry cannellini beans

4 oz salt pork, diced

4 chicken legs

4 chicken thighs

12 oz beef kielbasa, sliced ¼ inch thick

1 onion, diced

2 stalks celery, diced

1 shallot, minced

2 cloves garlic, minced

2 plum tomatoes, diced

1 cup white wine

1 qt. chicken stock

1 sprig sage

1 bay leaf

1 lb pork tenderloin, cubed

salt, to taste

ground black pepper, to taste

parsley, chopped, for serving

DIRECTIONS

1. In the Stock Pot, add the ham hock and beans, fill the pot with water, and simmer on the stove top for 1 hour.

2. In the High-Sided Fry Pan, add the salt pork and render over medium heat on the stove top.

3. Add the chicken and pan sear until golden. Remove and reserve the chicken.

4. Add the kielbasa and sear until golden brown. Remove and reserve the kielbasa.

5. Add the onion, celery, shallot, and garlic and sauté until tender.

6. Add the tomatoes and sauté for 3 minutes.

7. Add the wine and reduce by half.

8. Pour the vegetables into the Stock Pot. Add the chicken, kielbasa, stock, sage, bay leaf, and pork and simmer for 1 hour. Cook until the beans are creamy and the liquid is absorbed. Season with the salt and black pepper.

9. Serve the Cassoulet with the chopped parsley.

TIP: Soak the beans overnight to cook the beans faster. You can also use bacon instead of salt pork.

Pork Stew with Sweet Potatoes & Prunes

SERVES 6

INGREDIENTS

2 pork tenderloins, cubed

1 tsp. salt

½ tsp. ground black pepper

2 tbsp. olive oil

1 onion, diced

10 cremini mushrooms, quartered

1 shallot, minced

3 white carrots, cut into large chunks

3 tbsp. butter

3 tbsp. flour

½ cup Marsala wine

2 cups chicken stock

8 prunes, quartered

3 sweet potatoes, cubed

1 sprig tarragon

1 bay leaf

salt, to taste

ground black pepper, to taste

DIRECTIONS

1. Season the pork with the salt and black pepper.

2. In the High-Sided Fry Pan, heat the olive oil over medium-high heat on the stove top. When the oil is hot, brown the pork lightly. Remove and reserve the pork.

3. Sauté the onion, mushrooms, shallot, and carrots for 5–8 minutes.

4. Melt the butter in the pan. Stir in the flour and cook for 3 minutes.

5. Add the wine and stock and cook until creamy.

6. Add the pork, prunes, potatoes, tarragon, and bay leaf. Cover the pan with its lid and simmer for 40 minutes.

7. Season with the salt and black pepper before serving.

TIP: For a twist on this recipe, you can use dried apricots instead of prunes and switch the marsala to Riesling wine.

Grains & Vegetables

*Pictured here

Broccolini with Garlic & Olive Oil

SERVES 2

INGREDIENTS

1 tbsp. salt

1 bunch broccolini

2 tbsp. extra virgin olive oil

2 cloves garlic, sliced

½ tsp. sea salt

¼ tsp. ground black pepper

DIRECTIONS

1. Fill the Stock Pot with water. Add 1 tbsp. salt and bring to a boil over high heat on the stove top. When the water is boiling, blanch the broccolini for about 3 minutes. Then, remove the broccolini from the water and drain in the Crisper.

2. In the Fry Pan, heat the extra virgin olive oil over medium heat on the stove top. When the oil is hot, sauté the garlic until golden.

3. Add the broccolini and cook to heat.

4. Toss with the sea salt and black pepper before serving.

TIP: Instead of broccolini, you can also use broccoli or broccoli rabe.

Potato Galette

SERVES 6

INGREDIENTS

2 tbsp. butter

1 large onion, sliced

2 tbsp. olive oil

5 yellow medium-size potatoes, sliced thinly

1 tsp. salt

½ tsp. ground black pepper

chives, for garnish

sour cream, for serving

DIRECTIONS

1. In the Fry Pan, melt the butter over medium heat on the stove top. When the butter is melted, caramelize the onion. Remove and reserve the onion.

2. Preheat the oven to 350° F/177° C.

3. In the Fry Pan, add the olive oil and layer the potatoes in a spiral one layer a time with the caramelized onion between each layer. Cook over medium heat on the stove top for about 4 minutes.

4. Transfer the pan to the oven and cook until the potatoes are golden, crispy, and tender (about 40 minutes).

5. Let sit for 20 minutes before cutting and serving with the chives and sour cream.

TIP: For a twist on this recipe, you can use sweet potatoes or a mixture of both sweet and yellow potatoes.

Spaghetti Squash with
Shallots & Parmigiano Cheese

SERVES 6

INGREDIENTS

1 3-lb spaghetti squash, cut in half

1 cup water

¼ cup olive oil

1 shallot, minced

4 leaves sage, chopped

1 tsp. salt

½ tsp. ground black pepper

½ cup grated Parmigiano-Reggiano cheese

DIRECTIONS

1. Preheat the oven 425° F/218° C.

2. Place the spaghetti squash on a cookie sheet, cut side down. Add the water and bake in the oven until tender (about 30 minutes).

3. Remove the spaghetti squash from the oven and set aside until cool enough to handle. Then, scrape the squash from the shell using a fork so that it falls in thin strands.

4. In the High-Sided Fry Pan, heat the olive oil over medium-high heat on the stove top. When the oil is hot, add the shallot and cook for 2 minutes.

5. Add the spaghetti squash, sage, salt, and black pepper and stir. Cook until hot.

6. Add the cheese, toss, and serve.

TIP: Instead of roasting, you can microwave the spaghetti squash by piercing the skin and cooking on high for 5 minutes.

Spicy Szechuan Eggplant SERVES 4-6

INGREDIENTS

3 tbsp. grapeseed oil, divided

2 eggplants, cubed

2 cloves garlic, minced

2 tsp. minced ginger

3 scallions, chopped

SAUCE

¼ cup thick sweet soy sauce

1 tsp. sesame oil

1 tsp. chili paste

2 tbsp. rice wine

1 tbsp. cornstarch

3 tbsp. water

DIRECTIONS

1. In the High-Sided Fry Pan, heat 2 tbsp. grapeseed oil over high heat on the stove top. When the oil is hot, brown the eggplant for 4 minutes.

2. Cover the pan with its lid and cook for 2–3 minutes.

3. Remove the lid and make a space in the middle of the eggplant. Add 1 tbsp. grapeseed oil and the garlic, ginger, and scallion and sauté for 3 minutes. Then, toss together.

4. In a bowl, add the Sauce ingredients and mix well. Pour the Sauce over the eggplant and toss a few times until thick.

5. Serving suggestion: Serve as a side.

Shredded Brussels Sprouts SERVES 4

INGREDIENTS

6 strips bacon, diced small

½ lb Brussels sprouts, shredded

1 shallot, minced

½ tsp. salt

¼ tsp. ground black pepper

DIRECTIONS

1. In the High-Sided Fry Pan, sauté the bacon over medium-high heat on the stove top until crispy.

2. Add the Brussels sprouts and shallot and sauté until tender.

3. Season with the salt and black pepper before serving.

Cauliflower Rice Pilaf   SERVES 6

INGREDIENTS

1 head cauliflower or
3 cups of cauliflower rice

2 tbsp. butter

½ onion, diced small

1 clove garlic, minced

1 sprig rosemary

½ cup chicken or
vegetable broth

DIRECTIONS

1. Break the cauliflower up into florets. Pulse the cauliflower in a food processor until the cauliflower looks like rice.

2. In the Fry Pan, melt the butter over medium heat on the stove top. When the butter is melted, add the onion and garlic and cook for 2–3 minutes.

3. Add the cauliflower rice, rosemary, and broth and cook until all the liquid is gone.

4. Serving suggestion: Serve instead of rice.

Quinoa Salad   SERVES 6

INGREDIENTS

1 cup quinoa

2 cups water

½ tsp. salt

3 scallions, chopped

2 carrots, diced small

1 clove garlic, minced

1 red pepper, diced small

⅓ cup extra virgin olive oil

3 tbsp. white balsamic vinegar

2 tbsp. chopped basil

½ cup sliced almonds, toasted

salt, to taste

ground black pepper, to taste

DIRECTIONS

1. In the Sauce Pot, add the quinoa, water, and salt. Cover the pot with its lid and bring to a boil on the stove top. Then, lower to a simmer and cook until done (about 20 minutes). Let cool.

2. In a large bowl, add the quinoa, scallions, carrots, garlic, red pepper, extra virgin olive oil, vinegar, basil, and almonds and toss.

3. Season with the salt and black pepper before serving.

Beets & Apple Salad

SERVES 6

INGREDIENTS

1 bunch red beets

1 bunch yellow beets

¼ cup olive oil

½ cup red wine vinegar

1 shallot, minced

1 tsp. salt

½ tsp. ground black pepper

SALAD

1 red onion, sliced

1 Granny Smith apple,
cored & sliced

2 tbsp. white balsamic vinegar

¼ cup extra virgin olive oil

1 tbsp. chopped cilantro

½ tsp. sea salt

¼ tsp. ground black pepper

DIRECTIONS

1. Preheat the oven to 400° F/204° F.

2. In the High-Sided Fry Pan, add the beets, olive oil, red vinegar, shallot, salt, and black pepper. Cover the pan with its lid and transfer the pan to the oven. Roast until the beets are tender (about 1 hour).

3. When the beets are cool enough to peel, peel and slice the beets.

4. In a large bowl, toss the beets with the Salad ingredients and serve.

TIP: Instead of roasting both beets, you can simmer the red beets in the Sauce Pot with 1 tbsp. vinegar and roast the yellow beets.

Escarole & Beans

SERVES 4

INGREDIENTS

3 tbsp. extra virgin olive oil

½ onion, chopped small

3 cloves garlic, sliced thinly

1 head escarole, cleaned

15 oz canned cannellini beans, drained & rinsed

¼ cup white wine

½ tsp. sea salt

1 pinch red pepper flakes

DIRECTIONS

1. In the High-Sided Fry Pan, heat the extra virgin olive oil over medium heat on the stove top. When the oil is hot, sweat the onion and garlic until slightly golden.

2. Raise the heat to high. Add the escarole. Cover the pan with its lid and sauté the escarole until tender (about 5 minutes).

3. Add the beans and white wine and stir. Cook until heated through. Season with the salt and red pepper flakes.

TIP: You can use chicken or vegetable stock instead of wine.

Pearl Couscous Salad

SERVES 6

INGREDIENTS

1 ½ cups pearl couscous

1 ¾ cups water

1 pinch of salt

3 tbsp. chopped mint

1 clove garlic, minced

½ cup crumbled feta

1 cup small-diced cucumber

1 cup quartered grape tomatoes

¼ red onion, diced small

¼ cup pine nuts, toasted

2 tbsp. red wine vinegar

¼ cup extra virgin olive oil

½ tsp. sea salt

¼ tsp. ground black pepper

DIRECTIONS

1. In the Sauce Pot, add the couscous, water, and salt. Cover the pot with its lid and simmer on the stove top for 8 minutes. Then, let the couscous cool.

2. In a bowl, combine the mint, garlic, feta, cucumber, grape tomatoes, red onion, pine nuts, vinegar, extra virgin olive oil, salt, and black pepper. Toss with the cooled couscous and serve.

TIP: To make this dish more colorful, try using tri-color pearl couscous.

Dessert

*Pictured here

Sweet Beignets

MAKES 12 2 ½-INCH BEIGNETS

INGREDIENTS

vegetable oil, for frying

3 ½ cups flour,
plus more for rolling

1 ½ tsp. cream of tartar

½ tsp. baking soda

½ tsp. nutmeg

¼ tsp. salt

1 cup sugar

4 large eggs, lightly beaten

⅓ cup vegetable
shortening, melted

⅓ cup milk

¾ tsp. grated lemon rind

powdered sugar in a
sugar shaker, for serving

DIRECTIONS

1. Fill the High-Sided Fry Pan halfway with the vegetable oil. Heat the oil over medium-high heat until the oil reaches 365° F/185° C.

2. In a bowl, sift together 3 ½ cups flour, cream of tartar, baking soda, nutmeg, and salt.

3. In a large bowl, whisk together the sugar and eggs. Stir in the melted shortening, milk, and lemon rind.

4. Use a wooden spoon to stir the dry ingredients into the egg mixture until a biscuit-like dough forms.

5. Lightly flour a work surface and turn out the dough. Pat the dough out to a ¼ inch-thick round. Use a 2 ½–3-inch biscuit cutter to cut rounds out of the dough. Reroll the scraps.

6. When the oil is hot, fry the beignets in the Fry Pan until golden, turning several times to brown evenly (about 4 minutes). Use a slotted spoon to remove the beignets gently. Drain thoroughly on paper towels.

7. Shake the powdered sugar over the beignets and serve immediately.

TIP: Stale leftover beignets work great as an ingredient in bread pudding.

Chocolate Fudge with
Marshmallow & Caramel Drizzle   SERVES 4-6

INGREDIENTS

⅓ cup milk

½ cup sugar

1 stick butter, salted

8 oz semisweet chocolate, chopped

12 large marshmallows

¼ cup caramel sauce

¼ cup sliced almonds, toasted

DIRECTIONS

1. In the Sauce Pot, heat the milk, sugar, and butter over medium-high heat on the stove top. When the butter is melted, add the chocolate and stir until incorporated.

2. Pour the fudge into a parchment paper-lined 9 x 7-inch casserole and cake pan.

3. Place three rows of marshmallows, with four marshmallows in each row, on top of the fudge.

4. Drizzle the caramel sauce over the fudge and sprinkle the almonds over the fudge.

5. Refrigerate for 3 hours before cutting and serving.

TIP: Add leftover chopped fudge to the Strawberry Ice Cream recipe after you freeze it in an ice cream maker.

Skillet Butter Cake

SERVES 8

INGREDIENTS

BATTER

1 ½ cups butter, softened

2 ½ cups sugar

5 large eggs

4 ½ cups flour

1 tbsp. vanilla extract

2 tsp. baking powder

¾ tsp. baking soda

1 tsp. salt

1 ½ cups buttermilk

GLAZE

½ cup butter

1 cup sugar

3 tbsp. water

2 tsp. vanilla extract

DIRECTIONS

1. Preheat the oven 350° F/177° C

2. In a bowl, cream the softened butter and 2 ½ cups sugar together.

3. Add 1 egg at a time until mixed.

4. Add the flour, 1 tbsp. vanilla, baking powder, baking soda, salt, and buttermilk and mix until creamy.

5. Pour the batter into the High-Sided Fry Pan. Bake in the oven until a tester comes out clean (40–50 minutes).

6. When the cake is done cooking, let cool. Carefully remove the cake from the pan and place on a large platter.

7. In the Sauce Pot, melt the butter with 1 cup sugar over medium-high heat on the stove top. When the butter is melted, add the water and 2 tsp. vanilla to make the Glaze.

8. Use a straw to poke a few holes over the entire cake. Pour the hot glaze over the cake and serve.

TIP: Serve with toasted almonds for an added crunchy texture.

Strawberry–Rhubarb Crisp SERVES 8

INGREDIENTS

1 ½ lb rhubarb,
peeled & chopped

8 cups strawberries, halved

¾ cup sugar

2 tbsp. cornstarch

zest of ½ lemon

¼ tsp. cinnamon

CRUMB TOPPING

2 ½ cups flour

1 ½ cups brown sugar

¼ cup plus 2 tbsp. butter

1 tsp. cinnamon

DIRECTIONS

1. Preheat the oven to 375˚ F/191˚ C.

2. In a bowl, toss the rhubarb, strawberries, sugar, cornstarch, lemon zest, and cinnamon.

3. Pour the mixture into the High-Sided Fry Pan. Bake in the oven for 20 minutes.

4. In a bowl, mix all the Crumb Topping ingredients by hand until the mixture reaches a crumb-like texture.

5. Top the mixture in the pan with the Crumb Topping.

6. Return the High-Sided Fry Pan and bake for another 15 minutes.

7. Serving suggestion: Serve with ice cream.

TIP: To make this recipe all year round, you can use frozen rhubarb instead of fresh rhubarb.

Apple Tarte Tatin

SERVES 6

INGREDIENTS

¼ cup butter

½ cup brown sugar

¼ tsp. cinnamon

juice of ½ lemon

5 Granny Smith apples, peeled & sliced into 1 ½-inch pieces

1 sheet puff pastry, cut into a 11" circle

DIRECTIONS

1. Preheat the oven to 400° F/204° C.

2. In the Fry Pan, melt the butter over medium-low heat on the stove top. When the butter is melted, add the brown sugar, cinnamon, and lemon juice. Add the apples in a circle and cook for about 8 minutes.

3. Top with the puff pastry and tuck in the sides around the apples. Make six 1-inch slits in the puff pastry.

4. Transfer the pan to the oven and cook until the puff pastry is golden.

5. Remove the Apple Tarte Tatin from the pan by covering the pan with a plate and carefully flipping the pan over so the Apple Tarte Tatin ends up on the plate with the apples on top.

TIP: For a twist on this recipe, use pears instead of apples and follow the recipe's directions. Instead of the lemon, use ½ tsp. cardamom to season the pears.

Mixed Berry Pie

SERVES 8

INGREDIENTS

PIE CRUST

4 cups flour

2 tbsp. sugar

½ tsp. salt

1 ½ cups shortening

12 tbsp. water, extra cold

FILLING

1 lb strawberries, frozen

1 lb blackberries, frozen

1 lb blueberries, frozen

½ cup sugar

½ tsp. cinnamon

1 tsp. lemon zest

2 tbsp. cornstarch

EGG WASH

1 egg yolk

2 tbsp. milk

DIRECTIONS

1. Make the Pie Crust: In a mixing bowl, combine the flour, 2 tbsp. sugar, and ½ tsp. salt and mix well.

2. Add the shortening and mix until the mixture resembles coarse crumbs.

3. Add the water and let sit for 1 minute.

4. Use your hands or a fork to press the mixture together carefully to form two soft balls. Wrap the dough in plastic wrap and refrigerate for at least 30 minutes.

5. Remove the dough from the refrigerator and place it on a lightly floured surface. Roll the dough into two circles about 12 inches in diameter and ¼ inch thick. Gently fold the dough circles in half and then fold in half again so that you can lift it without tearing. Place one Pie Crust in a pie plate.

6. Make the Filling: In the High-Sided Fry Pan, add the frozen fruit, sugar, cinnamon, and lemon zest. Cook over medium heat on the stove top until the fruit starts to thaw.

7. Sprinkle the cornstarch over the fruit and bring to a boil. When boiling, remove from the heat and let cool.

8. Preheat the oven to 350° F/177° C

9. Pour the Filling into the pie plate.

10. In a bowl, beat together the yolk and milk to make the Egg Wash.

11. Cut the second Pie Crust into strips. Use the strips to make a lattice over the Filling. Brush with the Egg Wash and transfer the pan to the oven. Cook until the pie is golden brown (45 minutes–1 hour).

Skillet Peach Cobbler

SERVES 6

INGREDIENTS

10 peaches, peeled & sliced

¼ cup sugar

1 tbsp. cornstarch

½ tsp. cinnamon

DOUGH

½ cup butter

2 cups flour

⅓ cup sugar

1 pinch salt

2 tsp. baking powder

½ tsp. cinnamon

1 large egg

¾ cup buttermilk

DIRECTIONS

1. Cut an X shape in the bottom of each peach.

2. Fill the Stock Pot with water. Bring to a boil on the stove top.

3. Fill a large bowl with ice and water.

4. Place the peaches in the boiling water for about 1 minute. Then, transfer the peaches to the ice water. Peel, pit, and slice the peaches.

5. In the Fry Pan, add the peaches, ¼ cup sugar, cornstarch, and ½ tsp. cinnamon and cook over high heat on the stove top until slightly thickened (about 5 minutes).

6. Preheat the oven to 350° F/177° C.

7. In a bowl, combine the butter and flour. Use a fork or dough cutter to break the butter into pieces. Then, add ⅓ cup sugar, salt, baking powder, and ½ tsp. cinnamon.

8. In a dish, beat the egg with the buttermilk. Pour into the flour mixture and mix until incorporated. Spoon on top of the peaches.

9. Transfer the Fry Pan to the oven and bake until the dough is cooked and golden (20–30 minutes).

TIP: If you don't want to spend the time peeling the peaches, you can use nectarines or plums instead.

Coconut Cream Pie

SERVES 6-8

INGREDIENTS

PIE CRUST

2 cups all-purpose flour, plus more for working dough

1 tbsp. sugar

¼ tsp. salt

¾ cup solid vegetable shortening

6–7 tbsp. water, ice cold

FILLING

¾ cup sugar

1 ½ cups unsweetened coconut milk

1 ½ cups whole milk, divided

¼ cup cornstarch

5 egg yolks

1 tsp. salt

1 cup flaked, unsweetened coconut

2 tsp. vanilla extract

1 tbsp. butter

FOR SERVING

⅓ cup toasted coconut

whipped cream

DIRECTIONS

1. In a mixing bowl, combine the flour, 1 tbsp. sugar, and ¼ tsp. salt and mix well.

2. Add the shortening and mix until the mixture resembles coarse crumbs.

3. Add the water and let sit for 1 minute.

4. Use your hands or a fork to press the mixture together carefully to form a soft ball. Wrap the dough in plastic wrap and refrigerate for at least 30 minutes.

5. Remove the dough from the refrigerator and place it on a lightly floured surface. Roll the dough into a circle about 12 inches in diameter in ¼ inch thick. Gently fold the dough circle in half and then fold in half again so that you can lift it without tearing.

6. Unfold the dough into a pie plate. Crimp the edges and refrigerate again for 30 minutes before baking.

7. Preheat the oven to 350° F/177° C.

8. Line the dough with foil or parchment paper. Top with pie weights or beans so that the dough does not puff up.

9. Bake the pie shell in the oven until golden (25–30 minutes). Remove and let cool completely.

10. In the Sauce Pot, combine ¾ cup sugar, coconut milk, and 1 cup milk. Scald the mixture over medium heat on the stove top.

11. In a small mixing bowl, whisk together ½ cup milk and the cornstarch to make a slurry.

12. In a medium-size bowl, whisk together the yolks and 1 tsp. salt. Temper the yolks by adding ½ cup scalded milk mixture to the yolks and whisk well.

13. Add the yolk mixture and slurry into the Sauce Pot and whisk vigorously over medium heat on the stove top until thickened (about 2 minutes).

14. Remove the Sauce Pot from the heat and add the coconut, vanilla, and butter. Whisk until uniformly incorporated.

15. Pour the filling into the Pie Crust. Cover the pie with plastic wrap and refrigerate until chilled completely (about 2 hours).

16. Top with toasted coconut and a dollop of whipped cream before serving.

TIP: You can buy ready-made pie shells in the freezer section of the grocery store. Bake and pour the hot custard into the pie shells.

Chocolate Cream Pie

SERVES 6

INGREDIENTS

GRAHAM CRACKER PIE CRUST

1 ¼ cups graham
cracker crumbs

¼ cup sugar

¼ cup plus
1 tbsp. unsalted butter

CHOCOLATE PUDDING

2 cups
plus 2 tbsp. whole milk

½ cup sugar

5 oz semisweet
chocolate, chopped

3 egg yolks

2 tbsp. cocoa powder

2 tbsp. cornstarch

½ tsp. vanilla extract

2 tbsp. butter

2 cups sweetened
whipped cream

2 oz chocolate curls,
for garnish

DIRECTIONS

1. Preheat the oven to 375° F/191° C.

2. To make the Graham Cracker Pie Crust: In a bowl, combine the graham cracker crumbs and ¼ cup sugar.

3. In the Sauce Pot, melt the butter over medium heat on the stove top. When the butter is melted, add the butter to the Graham Cracker Pie Crust and stir well to combine.

4. Place the Graham Cracker Pie Crust in a pie pan and press the crust into the pan and up the sides of the pan. Bake the Graham Cracker Pie Crust in the oven until slightly golden (7–10 minutes).

5. To make the Chocolate Pudding: In the Stock Pot, add 2 cups milk and ½ cup sugar and bring to a boil over high heat on the stove top. When the sugar is dissolved, reduce the heat to medium-low.

6. Add the chocolate pieces and whisk until the chocolate is completely melted.

7. In a small bowl, whisk the yolks together. Temper the yolks into the chocolate mixture.

8. In a separate small bowl, whisk 2 tsp. milk and the cornstarch together to make a slurry. Slowly add the slurry into the hot chocolate mixture and mix well to blend. Bring the mixture to a boil and cook while stirring constantly until the mixture is thickened.

9. Remove the Stock Pot from the heat and stir in the vanilla and 2 tbsp. butter.

10. Pour the pudding over the Graham Cracker Pie Crust. Cover the pudding with plastic wrap to prevent the pudding from forming a skin. Refrigerate for 2–3 hours.

11. Top the pie with the whipped cream and garnish with the chocolate curls before serving.

Strawberry Ice Cream

SERVES 6-8

INGREDIENTS

1 qt. heavy cream

1 vanilla bean, sliced lengthwise

1 cup sugar, divided

10 egg yolks

4 cups strawberries,
pulsed in a food processor

DIRECTIONS

1. In the Stock Pot, add the heavy cream, vanilla, and ½ cup sugar. Bring to a boil on the stove top.

2. In a large bowl, add the yolks and ½ cup sugar and whisk to combine. Add 1 cup of the hot cream while whisking the egg yolks in the bowl. Repeat the hot cream addition twice more. Then, add the rest of the hot cream and whisk.

3. Remove the vanilla bean and use a paring knife to scrape the inside of the bean. Place the pulp into the cream and whisk.

4. Strain through a fine mesh strainer.

5. Add the strawberries and refrigerate until cooled (at least 2 hours).

6. Transfer the ice cream to an ice cream maker to freeze. When done, transfer to a freezer to freeze more before serving.

TIP: Add chopped-up vanilla wafers and top with whipped cream to make a mock strawberry shortcake.

Bananas Foster Crepes

SERVES 6

INGREDIENTS

CREPE BATTER

¾ cup all-purpose flour

3 large eggs, beaten

¾ cup plus 3 tbsp. whole milk

1 pinch salt

6 tsp. unsalted butter, melted, divided

FILLING

¼ cup plus 2 tbsp. butter

1 ¼ cups lightly packed brown sugar

¾ tsp. ground cinnamon

6 bananas, cut in half lengthwise, then half again crosswise

½ cup dark rum

_____

vanilla ice cream

DIRECTIONS

1. To make the Crepe Batter: In a bowl, whisk together the flour, eggs, milk, salt, and 4 ½ tsp. butter to form a smooth, thin batter. Refrigerate for at least 1 hour.

2. Heat the Fry Pan over medium-high heat on the stove top. When the pan is hot, brush the pan with a light coating of the remaining 1 ½ tsp. melted butter. Ladle about ¼ cup Crepe Batter into the pan, tilting and swirling the pan to evenly coat with the batter. Cook until golden brown on the bottom and the top begins to look dry (1–2 minutes).

3. Use a spatula to turn the crepe carefully and cook on the other side until the bottom colors slightly (about 30 seconds).

4. Transfer to a plate and cover loosely with wax paper to keep warm. Repeat until all the batter is used, brushing the pan lightly each time with some of the butter.

5. To make the Filling: In the High-Sided Fry Pan, melt the butter and brown sugar together on the stove top. Add the cinnamon, stir well, and cook for a few minutes.

6. Add the bananas and sauté until slightly soft, spooning the sugar mixture over the bananas to coat.

7. Carefully add the rum and flame.

8. Once the flames have died out, carefully remove the bananas from the pan and fold them into the crepes.

9. Top with a scoop or two of ice cream. Spoon the hot sauce over the ice cream and crepes.

Pear Upside-Down Cake SERVES 6

INGREDIENTS

3 tbsp. butter

⅓ packed cup brown sugar

3–4 pears, peeled,
cored & sliced

BATTER

5 tbsp. butter

½ cup granulated sugar

2 large eggs

1 tsp. vanilla extract

⅓ cup milk

1 ¼ cups flour

1 tsp. baking powder

1 pinch salt

_____

ice cream or whipped cream,
for serving

DIRECTIONS

1. Preheat the oven to 350° F/177° C.

2. In the Fry Pan, melt 3 tbsp. butter over medium-high heat on the stove top. When the butter is melted, add the brown sugar and pears and cook for 3 minutes.

3. Use a stand mixer to cream 5 tbsp. butter. Add the granulated sugar and mix.

4. Add 1 egg at a time and beat well.

5. Add the vanilla, milk, flour, baking powder, and salt and mix.

6. Pour the batter over the pears in the Fry Pan. Transfer the pan to the oven and bake until done (30–40 minutes).

7. Let cool slightly. Then, flip the pan onto a plate. Cool and serve with ice cream or whipped cream.

TIP: This recipe tastes best when you use in-season fruit. For example, you can use peaches or apples instead of pears.

Index

L

M

FOREVER PANS™